The Metaphysical and Geometrical
Doctrine of Bruno

A Monograph in

MODERN CONCEPTS OF PHILOSOPHY

Series Editor

MARVIN FARBER

State University of New York at Buffalo
Buffalo, New York

The Metaphysical and Geometrical Doctrine of Bruno

As Given in His Work

De Triplici Minimo

By

DR. KSENIJA ATANASIJEVIC

Belgrade-Paris
1923

Translated into English from the French Original

By

DR. GEORGE VID TOMASHEVICH

Professor of Anthropology
State University of New York
College at Buffalo

WARREN H. GREEN, INC.
St. Louis, Missouri, U.S.A.

Published by

WARREN H. GREEN, INC.
10 South Brentwood Boulevard
St. Louis, Missouri 63105, U.S.A.

© 1972 by WARREN H. GREEN, INC.

Library of Congress Catalog Card Number 76-155339

Printed in the United States of America

(193)

TRANSLATOR'S PREFACE

AND

ACKNOWLEDGMENTS

THIS VOLUME CONTAINS my translation from the French original of *Bruno's Metaphysical and Geometrical Doctrine, as Given in His Work "De Triplici Minimo"* (*La Doctrine Métaphysique et Géométrique de Bruno Exposée dans Son Ouvrage "De Triplici Minimo"*), a uniquely thorough exploration and critical analysis of a highly complex and previously neglected region of the greatest philosophical mind of the Renaissance by the eminent Yugoslav philosopher and classical philologist, Dr. Ksenija Atanasijevic.* Published simultaneously in Paris and Belgrade by *Les Presses Universitaires de France* and *Librairie "Polet,"*[1] respectively, this consummately documented appraisal of Bruno's pivotal place between his predecessors and successors in the history of philosophy and science in general, and of finitism in particular, appeared in 1923 as an early portent of its author's superb and prolific scholarship. The book's unusual worth and importance were quickly recognized and acclaimed by critics in Yugoslav as well as foreign journals. In the words of a London reviewer writing in the periodical *Nature* of August 15, 1925, "*La Doctrine Métaphysique et Géométrique de Bruno*, by Dr. Xénia Atanassievitch . . ., is not only a fascinating historical

---

* See "Biographical Note about the Author."

[1]*La Doctrine Métaphysique et Géométrique de Bruno Exposée Dans Son Ouvrage "De Triplici Minimo" par Xénia Atanassievitch, Docteur ès lettres,* Belgrade, *Librairie "Polet,"* "Imprimérie Mirototchivi" Rue Vouk Karadjitch, 26, 1923.

study of the great sixteenth-century pioneer of modern science but it is also of first-rate present scientific interest." The British scholar recalls, as a matter of course, that Dr. Petronijevic, whose theories about the discontinuity of space and time represent a further development of Bruno's finitism, is "the professor of philosophy at Belgrade, recently in Great Britain working at the reconstruction of Archaeopteryx."[2] The reviewer agrees that "there can be no doubt" about Bruno's writings having "influenced very definitely the mathematical and physical sciences in the seventeenth century" and finds it "of extraordinary interest to compare the unaided speculations of Bruno with the new form the theories assumed under the control of experiment." Evidently impressed by Dr. Atanasijevic's discussion of the extent of the Italian thinker's impact on subsequent movements of thought, the critic concurs that "all the distinctions which exercised the philosophers of the seventeenth century . . . are expounded in Bruno," and, to underscore the point, explicitly lists "the distinction between the mathematical, the physical and the metaphysical unit, the geometrical difficulty Descartes encountered in his conception of subtle matter and his rejection of the void, the difficulty for physics which Malebranche discovered in the idea of a minimum sensibile" and "the metaphysical difficulty Leibniz met with in relating God to the monads." In his conclusion, the London reviewer notes Dr. Atanasijevic's "valuable criticism which follows her able exposition."[3]

Most appropriately, an equally warm response came from Dr. Karel Vorovka, professor of philosophy at Charles' University in Prague, another major station in the great Nolan's itinerant career. Reviewing the book, in *Ruch Filosoficky* (*The Philosophical Herald*), *ročnik VI, čislo 4-6, 1926*, as "a very conscientious study," the Czech philosopher commends his Yugoslav colleague for devoting "full attention to particulars in a detailed

[2]For a list of publications by this internationally recognized Serbian philosopher, mathematician, and natural scientist, see *Résumé des Travaux Philosophiques et Scientifiques de Branislav Petronievics*, in *Bulletin de L' Académie des Lettres, Académie Royale Serbe*, Belgrade, 1937.

[3]See *Nature*, No. 2911, Vol. 116, London, Macmillan & Co., Ltd., Saturday, August 15, 1925, p. 257.

explication of Bruno's work *De Triplici Minimo et Mensura . . ."* and adds—with a ring of appreciation born, seemingly, of experience—that "the task is, indeed, not an easy one, but demands considerable patience, if one is to discern his ideas" through his "overabundant figures of speech" and other intricacies of his style. In the reviewer's opinion, "This is why, in the literature on Bruno, there has not been, until now, a single careful analysis of this work, so that, by writing her treatise, the author has earned great merit, for which every historian of philosophy must be thankful." Professor Vorovka seems particularly impressed by Dr. Atanasijevic's "historical chapter, where she expertly discusses the forerunners of Bruno's doctrine." He also praises "the author's abundant use of accurate evidence from original sources as well as of many literary references," and observes that "she has a masterly control of her material and knows how to give her philosophical studies a documentary value." The Czech reviewer concludes that "for everyone interested in the philosophy of mathematics, this study is a rich source in every respect, and not only from the historical point of view."[4]

The same year, the Italian specialist in the study of Bruno, Virgilio Salvestrini, included this remarkable monograph in his *Bibliografia delle opere di Giordano Bruno,* published in Pisa in 1926.[5] According to this bibliography's second posthumous edition, considerably enlarged by subsequent additions to the *Bruniana, La Doctrine Métaphysique et Géométrique de Bruno* was also reviewed by the Italian critic G. Loria, in *Scientia,* XLIV, 1928.[6] Besides, for more than a quarter of a century now, this singular work has been listed in the selected bibliography of major sources underlying the article on Bruno in the *Encyclopaedia Britannica.*

More recently, in a discussion of "Bruno and Science," in the Introduction to his translation of the Nolan's dialogues, *Della Causa, Principio e Uno,* Jack Lindsay rightly remarks that "his mathematics are often derided," but that "little work has

---

[4]See *Ruch Filosoficky,* rocnik VI, cislo 4-6, Praha, 1926, pp. 181-182.
[5]See his *Bibliografia delle opere di Giordano Bruno,* Pisa, 1926, p. 341.
[6]See Virgilio Salvestrini: *Bibliografia di Giordano Bruno* (1582-1950). Seconda edizione postuma a cura di Luigi Firpo. (*Biblioteca Bibliografia Italica, No. 12.*) Firenze: Sansoni Antiquariato, 1958.

been done on them," and adds: "The one exception is Xenia Atanassievitch's *La Doctrine Métaphysique et Géométrique de Bruno*, 1923, which is very respectful; she analyses his *Triple Minimum* and his position as a founder of discrete geometry."[7] It is a pity that, despite so clear a recognition of its significance in the critical literature on Bruno, this indispensable guide to a more precise understanding of his exact role as an anticipator and founder of modern philosophy and science does not appear in the "Brief list of Books on, or Connected with, Bruno," at the end of the volume.[8]

By contrast, *The Infinite Worlds of Giordano Bruno*,[9] a major work by Antoinette Mann Paterson, is both more extensive and more explicit in its acknowledgments: "For a valuable treatment of Bruno's theories on minima and monads"[10] Dr. Paterson refers the reader to Dr. Atanasijevic's treatise, as "the principal commentary" on Bruno's *De Triplici Minimo et Mensura.*[11] A formidable fighter in her own right for justice to Bruno at long last, Dr. Paterson is also the first American philosopher to try to render justice to Dr. Ksenija Atanasijevic: on more than one occasion she quotes her Yugoslav colleague[12] and lists four of her works in the bibliography.[13]

II

This translation owes its inception, on the one hand, to my own enduring interest in the Nolan's philosophy in general, and its inadequately examined anthropological implications in particular—an interest awakened years ago by my noble friend and inspiring teacher, Dr. Atanasijevic—and, on the other, to an academic encounter with Dr. Antoinette Mann Paterson, an American pioneer in the study of Bruno.

---

[7]See *Giordano Bruno, Della Causa, Principio e Uno*, Translated, with an Introduction, by Jack Lindsay, International Publishers, New York, 1964, p. 35.

[8]*Op. cit.*, pp. 176-177.

[9]See Antoinette Mann Paterson, *The Infinite Worlds of Giordano Bruno*, Charles C Thomas, Publishers, Springfield, Illinois, 1970.

[10]*Op. cit.*, p. 57.

[11]*Ibid.*, p. 81.

[12]*Ibid.*, p. 3 and pp. 9-10.

[13]*Ibid.*, p. 200.

In addition to my wholehearted thanks for her relentless insistence upon, abiding interest in, and manifold contribution to, the progress of my labor, Dr. Paterson deserves unqualified and exclusive credit for the very idea that this quintessential study of Bruno's Metaphysics and Geometry, available in French since 1923, should, almost half a century after its publication, become accessible in English.

To Dr. Lynn E. Rose, Professor of Philosophy at the State University of New York at Buffalo, I owe a debt of profound gratitude for placing at my disposal, among his other remarkable resources, the incisive and compelling logic of his critical reaction and advice, as well as for showing great kindness and painstaking attention to detail in proofreading and correcting virtually all of the semi-definitive text.

It gives me exceptional pleasure to acknowledge here, with warm thanks, a deep indebtedness to Diana and R. Joseph Myers, my dear friends and former students, without whose patient, conscientious and knowledgable assistance in more than one way the completion of this work would have been physically impossible. To Mr. and Mrs. Myers I am affectionately obligated not only for their generous gift of time, energy, intelligence and experience in typing and retyping several versions of the entire book, but also, to each individually, for many valuable editorial improvements and excellent stylistic touches.

I wish to express my appreciation also to my brother-in-law, Dr. Sherwood A. Wakeman, for many subtle, learned and well-taken objections to certain phraseological ambiguities in the first draft of the first chapter; to my sister, Mrs. Desa Tomašević-Wakeman, for a number of astute and felicitous suggestions of alternative terms in this Preface; and to my mother, Mrs. Mara Tomasevic, for tireless and intelligent assistance in checking and correcting the continuity of pagination as well as the footnotes.

Once again, I want to thank Dr. Ksenija Atanasijevic-Markovic, Dr. Milan Markovic and Prof. Ilinka Stankovic (Zora Djordjevic) for all their acts of kindness—too many and too varied to specify and enumerate—and Prof. Slobodan M. Petrovic for his courtesy in letting me consult the unpublished manuscript of his well documented and insightful essay on Dr. Ksenija

Atanasijevic, in which I found much of my factual information about her life and work.

Throughout this translation I have had the good fortune and privilege of being able to work very closely with the author of the original through frequent correspondence as well as in person, during my visits to Yugoslavia in the winter of 1968 and summer of 1969.

Finally, a special, cordial acknowledgment is due Miss Margo Skinner and Miss Sandee G. Schmidt for their understanding and attentive effort in retyping the whole manuscript in its definitive form.

In order to keep the price of this volume within reasonable limits and at the explicit request of the publisher, the extensive Greek and Latin passages occurring in footnotes of the author's French text are not reproduced here, but specific references to the original Greek and Latin sources—now easily accessible—are, naturally, always provided. In no other respect does this English translation depart from the French edition.

I alone, of course, bear the full responsibility for the accuracy and faithfulness of the translation itself as well as for any errors and imperfections that may have escaped scrutiny and detection.

In closing this Preface, I am particularly delighted that my translation of this work on Bruno by one of Yugoslavia's most outstanding scholars should be presented to her American colleagues by Dr. Marvin Farber, whose long and distinguished record of contributions to serious philosophy speaks for itself.

GEORGE VID TOMASHEVICH,
Professor of Anthropology
State University of New York,
College at Buffalo

A BIOGRAPHICAL NOTE ABOUT THE
AUTHOR OF THE FRENCH ORIGINAL

Born on February 5, 1894, Dr. Ksenija Atanasijevic (Xénia Atanassievitch) graduated from the University of Belgrade in 1920 with a diploma in philosophy and classical languages. She did graduate work in the history of philosophy and prepared her doctoral dissertation at the Universities of Geneva and Paris, under Robin, Bréhier and Brunschvickg. On January 20, 1922, upon her return to the University of Belgrade, she became the first woman in the annals of that Institution to earn the Degree of Doctor of Philosophy. Her Committee included, among others, two internationally known members of the Serbian Academy: the philosopher, mathematician and naturalist, Branislav Petronijevic (Petronievics) and the physicist-astronomer, Milutin Milankovic.

Between 1923 and 1936, as a Lecturer and Docent at the University of Belgrade, she taught the history of ancient, medieval and modern philosophy as well as aesthetics. In the interwar period, although engaged in full-time teaching and writing, she often lectured publicly in Belgrade, Athens, Paris and other cities, not only on topics in pure philosophy, but also in the defense of peace and the rights of women. Revolted by man's inhumanity to man, she directed her formidable mind, remarkable eloquence and incomparable erudition against the evils of Naziism, racism, anti-Semitism and all other types of bigotry and oppression. In 1941, following Yugoslavia's occupation by the Axis powers, Dr. Atanasijevic was removed from the Inspectorate of Instruction in the Ministry of Education (to which she had been nominated in 1939) and arrested by the

Gestapo. After the War, in 1946, she was retired as Librarian of the National Library.

Her enormous and far-ranging bibliography, produced in the course of over half a century of creative labor and scattered through Yugoslav and foreign publications, consists, in addition to many original books and several volumes of translations, of nearly 400 essays, articles and reviews, embracing most of the major philosophical topics and intellectual and artistic figures from virtually every part of the world and period of history.

Her most significant works appeared in the following chronological order:

"Filozofija Sofista" ("The Philosophy of the Sophists"), in Misao (Thought), 16, X. Belgrade, 1922; *Brunovo Učenje o Najmanjem* (*Bruno's Doctrine of the Minimum*) Belgrade, 1922; *La Doctrine Métaphysique et Géométrique de Bruno*, Belgrade-Paris, 1923; *Eleacanin Parmenid–Tvorac Učenja o Bicu* (*Parmenides of Elea-Creator of the Doctrine of Being*), Belgrade, 1927; *Stara Grčka Atomistika* (*Ancient Greek Atomism*), Belgrade, 1927; *L'Atomisme d'Epicure*, Paris, 1928.

"Počeci Filozofiranja kod Grka" ("The Beginnings of Philosophising among the Greeks"), in *RAD, Journal of the Yugoslav Academy*, vol. 235, Zagreb, 1928; *Filozofski Fragmenti* (*Philosophical Fragments*) vol. I, Belgrade, 1929 and vol. II, Belgrade, 1930; "Hegel bei den Jugoslawen" ("Hegel among the Yugoslavs") in *Ruch filozoficky* (*The Philosophical Herald*), Prague, 1933; *Blaise Pascal*, Belgrade, 1935; *Penseurs Yougoslaves* (*Yugoslav Thinkers*), Belgrade, 1937 and *Smisao i Vrednost Egzistencije–Aksiološka Razmatranja* (*The Meaning and Value of Existence–Axiological Reflections*), Belgrade, 1968.

Besides, Dr. Atanasijevic translated into Serbo-Croatian Spinoza's *Ethics*, 1934; Adler's *Individual Psychology*, 1937; Plato's *Parmenides*, 1959 and Aristotle's *Organon*, 1965. Like her other renditions from half a dozen languages, these are accompanied by book-length introductory studies and expert critical commentaries.

Among her other significant essays are those on Socrates,

Democritus, Empedocles, Julian the Apostate, the Essenes, Appollonius of Tyana, Philo of Alexandria, Aurelius Augustinus, Maimonides, La Bruyère, Descartes, Lock, Kant, Schopenhauer, Nietzsche, Taine, Tolstoi, Spengler, Freud, Tagore, Ortega y Gasset and the Serbian Philosopher of History—Božidar Kneževic.

AUTHOR'S PREFACE TO THE ENGLISH
TRANSLATION OF THIS BOOK

IN RESPONDING WITH pleasure to the request of Dr. George Vid Tomashevich, translator of this French book of mine into English, that I write a Preface to the American edition, I find it necessary to point out a number of facts which in the study of Bruno's creative work must be taken into consideration especially today, when the entire world enthusiastically celebrates the magnificent and epochal conquest of the moon by the courageous American astronauts. For Giordano Bruno is an early forerunner of all contemporary investigators of the cosmos, who paid for his views, revolutionary for the age in which he lived, with a gruesome death. This is why it is our duty to recall gratefully and with deep respect the magnitude of the sacrifice made for modern science and the advancement of the life of all of us by this greatest thinker of the Renaissance, this trail-blazing pioneer to whom belongs the enormous credit for placing astronomy definitively on correct scientific foundations.

We firmly hope that the perseverant and carefully coordinated teamwork, without which such scientific and technical triumphs could not be achieved, will contribute to the development of even closer cooperation among the scientists of various countries in the exploration of the universe, investigation of the origin of life on earth, as well as clarification of many earthly phenomena. We believe that, through the good will of reasonable and enlightened people, this scholarly cooperation will, in the long run, grow into a common labor for the improvement of all human existence and, as such, become one of the factors conducive to the gradual realization of the highest objective of the evolution of mankind: the transcendence of all anti-natural and ethically impermissible discriminations among individuals, peoples and races; the removal of all occasions for collisions and wars among nations; the realization of that perpetual peace about which Immanuel Kant dreamed and wrote; as well as the assurance of economic well-being and intellectual enlightenment for all people and establishment of true brotherhood among them based on full respect for the dignity and freedom of every conscious human individual.

In the afterglow of these beautiful hopes, awakened in us by the spectacular successes in the exploration of space, it ought to be pointed out that it was Giordano Bruno who, with an inexhaustible energy, persisted in refuting the narrow-mindedly erroneous system of Aristotle and Ptolemy, according to which the earth was the center of a finite universe.

A fiery adherent of the Copernican system, Bruno, even before Galileo's discovery by telescope, complemented the Copernican teaching with the farsighted affirmation that fixed stars are also suns surrounded by planets and that our sun is one of innumerable suns in an infinite universe. These views of Bruno's were to be assessed by the terrified officials of the Inquisition as "altogether the most absurd of horrors" (*"horrenda prorsus absurdissima"*).

Before Bruno, the ancient Hellenic atomists, Democritus and Epicurus, asserted and tried to prove that, contrary to the primitive conceptions of antiquity about a finite cosmos, the universe was infinite. Fascinated by these doctrines, particularly by that of Epicurus according to which the infinite cosmos contains infinitely many worlds, Bruno, from his metaphysical and astronomical position and in a poetic transport, repeatedly asserted that in the infinite universe the center is everywhere and the circumference nowhere, and that in it all contradictions disappear. Carried by his far-ranging metaphysical exultation, Bruno felt love toward all things in the universe; hence the confining teaching of the Catholic Church—built on the foundations of Aristotle's and Ptolemy's systems—which with regard to the whole unfathomable cosmic endlessness took into consideration only the earth and man upon it, eventually struck him as unacceptable. By assuming such a position, Bruno decisively took a stand against the Scholastic view of the world, destroying its very foundations. Dazzled by his own realization that there are innumerable worlds, the Nolan was aware of the enormous significance of his discovery. No wonder he thought: If Christopher Columbus was so celebrated for having discovered a new part of this terrestrial world, how much more worthy of celebration is he who penetrated the sky and there discovered expanses without end!

In his philosophizing, full of revolutionary ideas, the Italian thinker also developed a theory about the infinity of time which, as a metaphysical, formal category consists of indivisible moments. And each of the moments of time is a middle point between two immeasurabilities. In these and in other conceptions of Bruno's it is quite possible, *mutatis mutandis,* to find early anticipations of certain famous theories of modern science.

But Bruno's contribution to the development of subsequent philosophy and modern astronomy is beyond proper evaluation not only in terms of his conception of the infinity of the universe; with his comprehensively conceived and elaborately argued doctrine of the triple minimum he is also one of the leading forerunners of later monadology, atomism and the teachings about the discontinuity of space, time, motion and geometrical bodies. To the doctrine of the triple minimum the philosopher devoted his work *De Triplici Minimo et Mensura,* which is surcharged with a complex and original, but sporadically very entangled, content.

Although the teaching that the addition of matter can proceed *ad infinitum* is one of the pillars of Bruno's system, he asserted in the other direction, that through the division of matter one does arrive at ultimate parts, not further divisible, the minima. A minimum is, for this thinker, the substance of things. Bruno's minimum is three-fold: the general, metaphysical minimum or monad, that is, the spiritual substance no further divisible; the physical minimum or atom, as the smallest substance of bodies; and, finally, the geometrical minimum or point. According to Bruno, the knowledge of the minimum is an indispensable condition for the understanding of metaphysics, the natural sciences and mathematics. The Pythagorean monad, analyzed to a greater depth, becomes in Bruno the basic metaphysical substance and the subtly dismembered atom of Democritus and Epicurus, the basic physical substance. In Leibniz' *Monadology* one can detect a direct influence of the Nolan's conception of the monad as the substance of all things, a conception which appeared so absurd to the judges of the Inquisition that they did not want to dwell upon it at all.

If one takes into account that Leibniz is one of the greatest thinkers and an eminent mathematician, it becomes clear how powerfully radiant was the influence of the philosophy of Giordano Bruno. And it cannot be contested that there is a genetic and historic connection between the atom of Democritus, Epicurus and especially Bruno, on the one hand, and the ever more perfect and elaborate contemporary atomic theory, on the other, a theory which, after the demolition of the classical notion of atomic stability by the French physicist Henri Becquerel and the discovery of radium by Pierre and Marie Curie, has started, in the works of Rutherford, Bohr, Heisenberg and other modern atomists, along a truly wondrous path to the fantastic benefit, but also to the possible destruction, of the human species. In no case, however, may it be forgotten that, beside Democritus and Epicurus, it was Bruno who laid the firm foundations upon which was to rise, in the course of time, the magnificent edifice of new atomic science.

In his refutation of Aristotle's supposition that space was divisible to infinity, the Italian philosopher's exceptional dialectical ingenuity accomplished a brilliant breakthrough. Namely, in his struggle against Aristotle, toward whom he felt an insurmountable aversion, Bruno succeeded in convincingly invalidating the Stagirite's famous argument against the possibility of space being discontinuous, that is, composed of indivisible points. Aristotle argued that, if this were possible, points, being without parts, would have to fall, on contact, into one another and, accordingly, the extension of space could not be realized. Bruno refuted this argument in an original and incontrovertible manner by making the distinction between the minima, which are the smallest parts, and the termini, which are not parts but limits separating the minima so that they cannot fall into each other. With this, the Nolan successfully removed the main logical obstacle in the way of extended space on which Aristotle had insisted. Besides, the Italian thinker thereby demonstrated that a finite quantity cannot be composed, either actually or potentially, of an infinite number of parts. This argumentation of Bruno's, superior to the deduction of the great logician, stands out as an accomplishment of capital value in the history of doctrines about the discontinuity of space.

By pointing out the complexity and non-uniformity of the ultimate parts of substance, Bruno revealed not only the unfailing correctness of his intuition but also the whole depth of his philosophical mind and thus became the illuminated precursor of later atomists and monadologists as well as the founder of geometrical finitism. Chronologically, *De Triplici Minimo et Mensura* is one of Bruno's latest works. The philosopher began to publish it in Frankfurt but, before correcting it and as if pursued by some fateful resolve, indifferent to danger, he left for Venice, where he had been called by the perfidious young nobleman Giovanni Mocenigo. This despicable informer had invited Bruno, ostensibly, to have him lecture on his philosophy but, actually, to lure the thinker back to his native land, from which he had had to flee, and hand him over to the Inquisition.

De Triplici Minimo et Mensura contains many unclear passages. Consistently developed metaphysical and geometrical deductions are interrupted in it by strange digressions and fanciful tirades. In general, many of Bruno's writings, excessively rich in contents and frequently permeated with a dramatic beauty, a flaming enthusiasm and an attractive freshness, do not always excel in the precision of their exposition. This thinker possesses an extraordinary capacity for direct elucidation of truths but is not always sufficiently rigorous when these truths have to be logically demonstrated. This applies particularly to his Latin works, which, full of new and daring views, would be even formally exquisite if they were clearer and more systematic. His Italian dialogues, however, have an attractive form, and it was no exaggeration that they were compared with the Dialogues of Plato and the Comedies of Aristophanes. These writings abound in poetic digressions, a vivid dramatic quality and an expressive satire.

In any event, one thing is certain: If the Inquisition had not managed to put its jackal's claws upon him when he was 44 and if he had not been burnt alive at the age of 52, Bruno would have left to humanity some more of his inspired and farsighted conceptions. But, languishing for years in the dungeons of the Inquisition, where he was not permitted to write any new works, this metaphysical poet of the infinite who, above all else, yearned for the freedom of thought, expression and creation (a freedom denied to many even today!) and who, together with the great representatives of early modern science, cut in their very roots the dessicated dogmas of Scholasticism, was compelled—in the hope of thus saving his life—to address to the deaf ears of the Inquisitors entire orations in which he presented his system in a condensed form.

In one of these orations he said: "I presuppose an infinite universe, a work of infinite Divine Power, because I consider it unworthy of the Divine Power and Goodness to produce only this world when it could have created infinitely many worlds similar to our earth, under which I understand, along with Pythagoras, a celestial body similar to the moon and other planets and stars. All these bodies are inhabited worlds, the immeasurable number of which, in the infinite space, forms an endless universe."

But all was in vain: To Bruno's insanely disposed and dogmatically fanaticized judges, the thinker who toppled the entire system of spheres of ancient astronomy (in anticipating the discoveries of Galileo, Kepler, Huygens, Newton and Herschel) and who, by his cosmocentric conception, transcended even the Copernican heliocentrism, appeared extremely dangerous. With a cretinism worthy of hyenas, they set out to ascertain how much blasphemy could be unearthed from a philosophy which was to fertilize directly and abundantly the systems of the most prominent later thinkers: Descartes, Leibniz, Spinoza, Berkeley, Schelling, Hegel, and the most reflective of the poets, Goethe. But, since after more than nine years of strenuous endeavor to wrangle Bruno out of his convictions, the "Holy"

Inquisition, despite its time-tested criminal experience and bestial skill in interrogating and hearing its victims, did not succeed in its "brotherly" attempt to make the thinker renounce his teaching, on February 8, 1600, it handed down the following verdict: The philosopher is guilty of having taught heretical theories which he was not willing to abjure. Having performed on the writer of *La Cena delle Ceneri* the dreadful ritual of deconsecration of a former monk, the ecclesiastical dignitaries "gave him over to the secular authority with the request that he be punished as mercifully as possible and without the shedding of blood" (*"seculari Magistratui eum tradiderunt puniendum rogantes, ut quam clementissime et sine sanguinis effusione puniretur"*). And this was the satanic formula for burning. Upon hearing the judgment pronounced, Bruno warningly exclaimed: "Perhaps your fear in passing this sentence upon me is greater than mine in accepting it." (*"Maiori forsan cum timore sententiam in me fertis, quam ego accipiam."*)

Of Bruno's burning the Inquisition made a monstrous spectacle, Rome being at that time full of Catholic pilgrims from all countries. In the early morning of February 17, 1600, a ghastly procession started from the prison of the Inquisition toward *Campo dei fiori*, in front of Pompey's theater. The author of the mystically poetic work *Degli Eroici Furori* ascended the stake with a firm step and a defiant expression and remained calm as they lighted it. After Bruno's body had burnt up, his ashes were scattered to the winds, so as not to leave on earth any trace of his corporeal shell. In 1603, all of the Nolan's works were placed by Rome on the Index of Forbidden Books (*Index Librorum Prohibitorum*). After being consigned to oblivion for all of two centuries, his writings, revived through the efforts of thoughtful and progressive people, became topical again and began to reappear in print.

But neither was the Inquisition completely vanquished. The depth of the roots which that hideous and malignant institution had extended into the minds of certain monsters in human shape can best be seen in the light of the fact that the dungeons for the unlikeminded and the placing of books on one index or another continue, indeed, even in our century!

Thus it was adjudged by fate that the enlightened philosopher who with his penetrating insight had encompassed the entire cosmos, celebrating its splendor and immeasurableness without dwelling upon particular ugly manifestions of painfully difficult human life, should spend his short career restlessly, in constant insecurity and disturbance, as well as incessant stormy migration and retreat before infernal enemies, to end his martyred life, at last, at a stake of the Inquisition. But after his death, this Italian thinker of genius, this "academician of no academy" (as he called himself), who was insulted, slandered and relentlessly persecuted in his lifetime, won fame and recognition for his teachings about an endless cosmos, about the prevalence of good over evil and about monads, atoms and minima.

The life of a thinker illuminates that which he created. For every philosophical structure is the highest expression of the being of its creator. Hence, Bruno's vast and fecund conceptions assume a scintillating attractiveness from his wondrously complex and overflowingly gifted personality which, in a period dominated by an obscurantist intellectual dogmatism and a fanatical, desperately sterile theological blindness, shone with the light of truth like those innumerable suns with which his visionary spirit filled the immeasurable universe.

For all these and other important reasons, the author believes that the publication of this excellent English version of her French work on Bruno's doctrine of the minimum represents, especially in the aftermath of man's landing on the moon, an event of indisputable philosophical and scientific interest and that, as such, it should be a welcome addition to the rapidly growing critical literature on the much calumniated and long-neglected philosophical and scientific genius from Nola.

To Dr. George Vid Tomashevich, our dear friend and former pupil, we feel obligated to express our warm gratitude for his indeed successful enterprise.

Dr. Ksenija Atanasijevic

INTRODUCTION

IT IS NOT OUR intention to make a study of the doctrines of all the representatives of finitism in ancient as well as modern philosophy. We have chosen as the subject of this study a special theory of finitism, namely, the doctrine of the minimum of Giordano Bruno, certainly the greatest philosopher of the XVIth Century.

On two points, the doctrine of Bruno differs essentially from that of Aristotle, in Bruno's estimate "the most stupid of all philosophers" (*"Stupidissimus omnium philosophorum"*).

First, Aristotle asserts, as does Ptolemy later, that in the center of the finite universe, bounded by the sphere of fixed stars, the earth stands motionless and all celestial bodies turn around it. Bruno, however, passionately adheres to the doctrine of Copernicus on which he bases his cosmology, and which, even before Galileo's discoveries by telescope, he enlarges with his assertion that fixed stars are also suns, surrounded, like our sun, by planets. Therefore, our sun being one of innumerable suns, the universe is infinite.[1] Secondly, Aristotle asserts that in the universe matter is divisible to infinity, that by its division one can in no way arrive at ultimate indivisible parts. Similarly, to Aristotle, time and space, although finite above, are divisible to infinity. According to Bruno, on the contrary, although the addition of material parts can be pursued *ad infinitum,* by subtraction one must arrive at ultimate parts which are not divisible any further. Thus, Aristotle represents the theory of the finite above and of the infinite below, while Bruno professes that of

---

[1] We point out in passing that many of Bruno's hypotheses about the structure of the universe can be regarded as anticipations of the results of modern natural sciences.

the infinite above and of the finite below: the infinite universe is the highest unity and the last of the infinite number of indivisible monads.

It seems to us that Bruno's theory as to the finite below is of very great importance and that its interpretation is as useful as that of his other philosophical ideas. But while Bruno's general philosophical conceptions have by now been commented on with success in numerous studies, his conception of the monad remains insufficiently treated. This is why Bruno is known above all for his ideas on the infinite in the universe and is almost unknown as defender of the finite in matter.

In his *Cena delle Ceneri* (*The Ash Wednesday Supper*, 1584) and *Spaccio della Bestia Trionfante* (*The Expulsion of the Triumphant Beast*, 1584) Bruno has left only a glimpse of his ideas about the last and indivisible parts of matter. In his *Acrotismus* (1588), however, he explicitly says the following: "The division of nature has a limit; there exists something indivisible; the division of nature attains the smallest and last parts which are not perceptible by man-made instruments.[2]" This idea is expounded by him in a concise and clear manner and in the same form as the theory already worked out in his *Articuli adversus Mathematicos* (*Articles against Mathematicians*, published in Prague in 1588). But his work *De Triplici Minimo et Mensura, ad Trium Speculativarum Scientiarum et Multarum Activarum Artium Principia* (*On the Threefold Minimum and Measure, as Principles of Three Speculative Sciences and Numerous Practical Arts*, Frankfurt, 1591) is especially devoted to the development of that doctrine.

Just as it is evident that the philosophy of Bruno synthesizes the doctrines of ancient philosophers (in the first place, the pre-Socratics: Pythagoras, Heraclitus, Parmenides, Zeno, Democritus, Empdeocles and then Epicurus and Plotinus), so it is equally evident that it contains the seeds of numerous systems of modern philosophy. It has been established that Descartes, Malebranche, Spinoza, Leibniz, Fichte, Schelling and Hegel were inspired by the ideas of Bruno. Bruno's doctrine of the minimum serves as a historical antecedent to two doctrines in particular:

[2]*Cam. Art.* 42, p. 154.

(1) Leibniz's Monadology and (2) the doctrine of space, includ-
the construction of a new geometry, by the contemporary finitist
Petronijevic.

Several authors have tried to throw light upon the relationship which exists between the system of Leibniz and that of
Bruno.[3] Nevertheless, this study is the first to note the historical
link between the fragmentary construction by Bruno of a
geometry simpler and more logical than the usual and the
geometrical system of Petronijevic.

A detailed interpretation of Bruno's metaphysical and mathematical doctrine of the minimum will serve as the focal point
of our exposé. Our purpose will be to relate the doctrine of
Petronijevic to that of Bruno and to infer conclusively the
measure in which Bruno is the predecessor of contemporary
finitism. The exposition will be based principally on *De Triplici
Minimo*, but *Articuli adversus Mathematicos* will be taken into
consideration whenever the assertions they contain are likely to
render clearer those in *De Triplici Minimo*.[4]

---

[3]In his *Histoire de la philosophie* Brucker indicates that Leibniz's system
depends on Bruno's conceptions, particularly those expounded in his work *De
Triplici Minimo* . . . (*Historia Philosophiae*, Vol. IV, p. 32 and further). Lacroze
emphasizes this dependence even more strongly . . . (Thes. epist. Lacrozian, Vol.
III, p. 78). In his dissertation, *Giordano Bruno's Lehre vom Kleinsten als die
Quelle der prästabilierten Harmonie von Leibniz, 1890*, Herman Brunnhofer
accuses Leibniz of having appropriated, in a somewhat modified form, Bruno's
ideas about the minimum. Dühring's accusation is even graver. In his *Kritische
Geschichte der Philosophie*, 1894, p. 336, this author speaks of "Leibnizens
eklektische Reflex-und Gelegenheits-philosopheme," and calls these "eine Verun-
staltung der Brunoschen Monadenlehre." Dühring goes even so far as to say:
"Ein Bruno hat sicherlich nicht davon geträumt, zu welchen Missgestaltungen
das, was er bei seinem Aufenthalt im Ländchen der Braunschweigischen Herzoge
am Abend seines Lebens erdacht hatte, stillschweigend ausgebeutet werden . . ."
(p. 348).—It goes without saying that these accusations have been leveled as a
result of a lack of understanding, for there is an enormous difference between
Bruno's hastily constructed hypotheses about the monad and Leibniz's logically
and systematically deduced Monadology.

[4]Until now, *De Triplici Minimo* has not been analyzed from the point of
view which is of interest to this author. In all the treatises dealing with the
philosophy of Bruno the subject of *De Triplici Minimo* is explained only in a
general manner. Brucker does expound the content of this work sufficiently,
but limits himself to Bruno's philosophical ideas; he does not even mention his
geometrical constructions (loc. cit.). In addition to an explication of Bruno's
philosophical views, K. Lasswitz, a rather able critic, also gives Bruno's geo-

Before proceeding to Bruno's doctrine of the minimum, we shall occupy ourselves with its precursors or, more closely, those who seem to us to merit this name. These are, in the first place, the Pythagoreans, then the atomists Leucippus and Democritus and, finally, the Arab scholastics, the Mutakallimun. At the same time, we shall cast a glance upon the development of the opposite theory, that of infinitism, in order to make our work clearer. Infinitism will evidently be treated only to the extent to which it may be useful to our subject, because the presentation of the whole development of the theory of continuity of space and matter and of the continuous geometry before Bruno would lead us too far afield and make us depart unduly from the outlined course.

---

metrical doctrine, but this explication is somewhat summary (*Geschichte der Atomistik*, Vol. I, pp. 359-401). Lewis McIntyre devotes a chapter of his documented study to Bruno's doctrine of the monads and atoms. He does not deal with the geometrical aspect of this doctrine but underscores its utility while emphasizing at the same time the difficulty of such an enterprise. "It is no part of the purpose of this book to go at length into the mathematics of Bruno, which unfortunately have not yet met with a competent exposition. Apart from the difficulty of the matter itself, the poetical form and setting of his theorems is an additional stumbling block in the way of understanding. Bruno was put to many shifts in order to give a poetical colouring to the most prosaic of subjects" (*Giordano Bruno*, London, 1903, Chapter V. p. 233).

CONTENTS

The Metaphysical and Geometrical
Doctrine of Bruno

Chapter I

FORERUNNERS OF BRUNO'S DOCTRINE OF THE MINIMUM

Aᴄᴄᴏʀᴅɪɴɢ ᴛᴏ ᴀʟʟ evidence, the Pythagoreans were the earliest forerunners of Bruno's theory of the minimum. This is why we shall examine their mathematical and philosophical teaching a little more minutely.

The fundamental idea of Pythagorean philosophy consists in the affirmation that number is the principle of things. To this idea the Pythagoreans were led by the study of mathematics and by the discovery of measure and of numbers in things themselves and in their relations to one another.[1]

The development of Pythagoreanism was rendered possible as a result of discoveries achieved in the domain of numbers themselves. The Pythagoreans studied the nature of square numbers; as a result, they established the difference between the even and the odd numbers, the simple and the composite ones.

For the Pythagoreans number is, then, the essence of things; everything is made of numbers; all is, in essence, number.

---

[1]Aristotle says that the Pythagoreans had devoted themselves to mathematics and had become so familiar with that science that they regarded mathematical principles as principles of being. Since, in accordance with the nature of things, numbers are that which is of principal importance in mathematics, and since the Pythagoreans thought they saw in numbers numerous resemblances to that which is and that which comes into being . . . seeing that everything seemed to be formed in accordance with number and that numbers had been acknowledged as that which is principal in all nature, they considered the elements of numbers to be the elements of all beings (of everything existent) and the entire heaven to be harmony and number. Cf. Greek text provided in the French original (*Met. A. 5, 985 b. 23*).

3

We shall merely mention two interpretations of the Pythagorean proposition that number is the principle of things. The first of these affirms that the Pythagoreans regarded number as the substance of things, the second, that they regarded number as the model on which things are constructed.

Without dwelling upon these interpretations, we shall say that Zeller's comment strikes us as well taken. According to Zeller, Aristotle presents the subject as if the Pythagoreans had taken things for copies of numbers because numbers, for them, would have been the beings that compose things; hence, the qualities of numbers must exist in things.[2]

Likewise, we shall not enter into an enumeration of the mathematical discoveries of the Pythagoreans which actually mark the formation of Greek mathematics; for Pythagoreanism is the first scientific doctrine of philosophy before Socrates. We are interested mainly in the Pythagoreans' attempt at constructing geometry from simple points as the first attempt of this kind in the history of human thought.

According to the Pythagoreans, the point (the monad, *monas*) is the principle of geometrical bodies. The point is the correlate of number. More exactly, it is a unit which has a position, a unit considered in space. From this very definition of the mathematical point, it follows that a solid body is a sum of such points, i.e., a sum of units. The elementary line is composed of two points situated one beside the other in such a manner that there is no third point between them. In the words of Aristotle, "They reduced everything to number and asserted that the notion of line is the notion of the number two."[3] The elementary space is composed of three lines and the elementary solid of four

---

[2]Eduard Zeller, *Die Philosophie der Griechen*, II, 4th edition, p. 319. See also G. Milhaud, *Les philosophes géomètres de la Grèce*, p. 105. "To the Pythagoreans number is not a transcendent reality, external to things modeled after it; it is immanent. They, indeed, talk much about imitation, *mimesis,* but the assertion which Aristotle repeats several times, that number is not separate (*horistos*), gives to this imitation a special sense: it is rather a sort of external reflection of an internal reality. It is difficult, moreover, to illuminate, with any precision, the relationship of things with regard to their first principle. After all, except for the prime mover, it is easy to find here all the forms of the causal relationship."

[3]Cf. Greek text provided in the French original (*Met. VII, 11, 1036 b. 7*).

surfaces. One can see, therefore, why the Pythagoreans identified the number *one* with a point, the number *two* with a line, the number *three* with a surface and the number *four* with a solid. Points (monads), that is to say, numbers, are the constitutive principles of lines, surfaces and solids. Consequently, the solid reduces itself in the end to points.[4]

The Pythagoreans must have been aware of the difficulty subsequently formulated by Aristotle, namely, that the line cannot be composed of points alone, because, if placed beside one another, they would coincide, and that, for the same reason, lines and surfaces themselves cannot compose surfaces and solids. This is why the Pythagoreans suppose that the points and the intervals (*diastemata*) between them constitute the condition for the existence of geometrical figures composed of points. Solids as well as musical harmonies are sums of units separated or linked by intervals. The points being identical with arithmetical units, one can say, by analogy with the foregoing, that a unit alone does not constitute number; in order that a unit may be linked to another unit, or other units, it is necessary that an interval exist between them. Intervals are the principle of plurality; more exactly, they are the principle of the infinite (*apeiron*), whereas, the points are the principle of the finite (*peras*). The unit is unpaired, and the first number greater than this unit, the dyad, is paired. Number consists, therefore, of both the unpaired and the paired (the odd and the even). Philolaus says: "Number, by its nature, has two forms which are proper to it; the even form and the odd form as well as a third form which results from the mixture of the preceding two, the even-odd form.[5] Each of these forms has numerous aspects, which every particular thing discloses in itself."[6] The even and the odd are general elements of numbers, that is to say, of things.

---

[4]"Some believe that the limits of solids, namely, the surface, line and point, are the substance, and that they are this more than are corporeal and extended things themselves." Cf. Greek text provided in the French original (*Arist. Met. VII*, 2. 1028 b. 16). See also *Met. XIII, 3. 1090 b. 5.*

[5]Even-odd (*artioperitton*) designates, assuredly, those even numbers which, divided by two, yield odd numbers.

[6]Cf. Greek text provided in H. Diels, *Die Fragmente der Vorsokratiker, tome I*, 1906, p. 240.

In the interpretation of the relation of the *apeiron* to number one can distinguish among the Pythagoreans two schools: the monists (represented by Pythagoras and the old Pythagoreans) and the dualists (represented by Philolaus). The monists considered *apeiron* as a principle existing in things themselves: the dualists believed it to be outside things.

According to the monists, *peras* (the limit, the finite) is the principle of the odd, while the *apeiron* (the infinite) is the principle of the even; both are principles of number. An odd number is limited in itself; it represents a whole which cannot be decomposed. An even number, however, consists of two halves which can be separated. For this reason, they identified the even with the infinite and the odd with the finite.[7] The Pythagoreans believed that all things contain opposites. They reduced all opposites to that between the finite and the infinite; more precisely, they gave to the finite and to the infinite different names: odd and even, one and multiple, right and left, male and female, rest and motion, straight line and curved line, light and darkness, good and evil, square and quadrangle.[8]

Here, the dualist doctrine is of particular interest to us. According to this doctrine, number in itself is the principle of the finite, more precisely, the finite proceeds from number. The infinite is an independent principle, it exists beside numbers. The infinite is identical with the void (*kenon*). The void separates all things and all numbers.[9] We have here, then, two principles: *the finite and empty space. Empty space, the place of figures, is the principle of continuity; the finite, that is to say number, is the principle of discontinuity.*

The origin of all that exists in space, of all bodies and all figures, is to be found in number. Space renders figures possible but it does not constitute them. Figures in space are constituted according to the principle of discontinuity. Bodies can be reduced to figures, they are composed of figures; figures are composed of numbers, in other words, of indivisible points.

---

[7]According to the Pythagoreans, number is the principle of being, just as well as matter and as quality and state; the elements of number are even and odd. The even is infinite, while the odd is finite. Cf. *Arist. Met. A, 5. 968 b. 6.*

[8]*Arist. Met. A, 5. 986 a. 22.*

[9]Cf. *Arist. Phys. IV, 6. 213 b. 22.*

Briefly, physical bodies can be reduced to solids, and solids to numbers. According to the dualists, *therefore, geometrical figures are identical with physical bodies which are composed of real points.*

The number one being the principle of all numbers, and all things being composed of numbers, one is the principle of all things.[10] Let us also say that for the Pythagoreans, the tetrad (four) is a mystical number; it is the source and origin or nature which undergoes perpetual change. In the Pythagorean arithmetic, the decad (ten) plays a very great role; on the one hand, it is the basis of the decimal system and, on the other, the sum of the first four numbers. Philolaus says with enthusiasm: "The activity and the essence of number must be evaluated by the power which is in the decad. For the decad is great, perfect, all-powerful; it is the beginning and the guide of divine, celestial and human lives . . . Without it, all is infinite, indeterminate and uncertain."[11] All numbers higher than the decad are but repetitions of the first ten numbers, because, in the opinion of the Pythagoreans, there are only ten numbers.[12] These symbolizations of certain numbers by the Pythagoreans have influenced Bruno, as we shall see.

Zeller doubts that Philolaus identified God with the number one.[13] It seems to us, nevertheless, that this is very possible, especially inasmuch as in Bruno, greatly inspired by Pythagoreanism, one encounters the identification of God with the monad.

The Pythagoreans explain the formation of ten cosmic bodies in a manner which is in perfect accord with the principles of their mathematical doctrine. If there existed only the principle of number, there would exist only one thing; there would be no plurality. In order that the existence of plurality be possible, there had to exist the principle of the void which is infinite and undivided, but has the power to divide. The void is infinite, contrary to the world which is finite. The original unit is in the center of the universe; it is the principle of the finite. This

[10]Cf. Diels, *op. cit.* p. 242.
[11]Cf. Diels, *op. cit.*, p. 243.
[12]Cf. *Arist. Met. XIII, 8. 1084 a. 12.*
[13]*Die Philosophie der Griechen,* p. 344.

original unit draws in the void in order to divide itself and create the world. In this manner, the void enters into the unit and divides it into a world of plurality.

The following passage from Philolaus will show how profoundly the Pythagoreans were affected by the idea that all earthly things and all celestial phenomena can be reduced to number and that number is the basis of everything: "For no thing would be clear, either in relation to itself or in relation to other things, if number and its essence did not exist."[14]

It is interesting to note that the Pythagoreans themselves gave the first construction of discontinuous geometry, in spite of the fact that they discovered the incommensurability of the side of a square and its diagonal. In the most harmonious figure, the square, they discovered a geometrical element which is not a sum of points. The incommensurable quantities should, precisely, have rendered impossible the fundamental postulate of their geometrical doctrine. But the Pythagoreans did not even try to resolve this difficulty, that is, to reconcile their geometry with the existence of incommensurable magnitudes.

The Pythagoreans were the first to think of unifying geometry as the science of space and arithmetic as the science of number. But a contradiction slipped into their geometric conception: the principle of continuity (empty space). That contradiction was sensed by Philolaus who said that falsehood is proper to the infinite, and that truth is proper to the finite, to number. "The nature of number and harmony do not partake of anything false because falsehood is not proper to them. Falsehood and envy are proper however to the nature of the infinite, the imprudent, the irrational."[15]

Although the Pythagorean conception of geometry has had great adversaries, from Aristotle to modern scholars,[16] it repre-

---

[14]Cf. Diels, *op. cit.*, from fragment 11, p. 243.

[15]From fragment 11, p. 244. Aristotle also says that, according to the Pythagoreans, the infinite is the evil and the finite the good. Cf. *Arist. Eth. N. II, 5. 1106 b. 29.*

[16]Aristotle considers it absolutely impossible for bodies to be composed of numbers, and for these numbers to be mathematical numbers. On the one hand, it is not possible to speak of indivisible quantities, and, on the other, even if they are possible, the units, certainly, are without size. "How is it possible for magnitude to be composed of indivisible parts? And despite this, the arithmetical

sents, nevertheless, an ingenious attempt at simplifying geometry and, in this quality, occupies an important place in the history of finitism.

The Eleatics represent a strong reaction against the Pythagorean conception of the discontinuous.

According to Parmenides, being fills up the entire space; consequently, non-being, which would be empty space without matter, does not exist. Nothingness being non-existent, there is nothing outside being. Being itself is homogeneous; it is spherical in form, that is to say, limited in all directions. Being is uniform throughout; it is not denser or rarer at places, for that would mean the existence of non-being; being is without voids and indivisible, for, if there were parts in being, between those parts

---

number is composed of indivisible units." Cf. *Met. XIII, 8. 1083 b. 18.* Paul Tannery is a declared adversary of the construction of solids from points, as taught by the Pythagoreans. He refutes the basic postulate of that construction, namely, the identification of the point with the unit. "Now, such a proposition is absolutely false; a body, a surface or a line are by no means a sum, a totality of juxtaposed points; the point, mathematically speaking, is in no way a unit; it is a pure zero, a nothing of quantity. That, despite the development of their geometrical knowledge, the Pythagoreans should have committed this error, one should not be astonished; they had started, as a matter of fact, from the vulgar prejudice, still shared by the majority of those unacquainted with mathematics, and the only discovery that could have made them suspect this prejudice, namely, the discovery of the existence of incommensurable quantities, had remained in their School, as the history of mathematics makes us realize, a veritable logical scandal and a formidable stumbling block" (*Pour la science héllène,* p. 251). G. Milhaud, who finds that the *Elements of Euclid* represent, apart from a few exceptions, the knowledge of the Pythagoreans, clearly marks the difference between the concept of the continuous, applied by Euclid in his geometry, and the concept of the discontinuous of the Pythagoreans. "In Euclid demonstrations are produced with an array of geometrical gear: numbers, whole numbers, are represented by lengths, and Euclid is arguing about geometrical figures; but in the *Elements* it is a geometrical magnitude, continuous length, line in the proper sense of the word, which serves to support the intuition. Tradition related to the Pythagorean arithmetic shows, on the contrary, geometrical figures being presented as aggregates of points. Here, lines are files of unit-points; a series of these lines will be able to form, for example, a triangle; a series of superimposed triangles will be able to form a pyramid, etc." (*Op. cit.,* p. 96-97). But he sees in the essential idea of the Pythagorean geometry also an error, later corrected by the definitive acceptance of the concept of continuity. "Nothing less will be necessary, to shake the naive representations of the first Pythagoreans, than the elaboration of the concept of mathematical continuum, an elaboration that will be made simultaneously under the influence of Eleatic thought and as a result of the natural advancements of geometry" (p. 110).

there would be non-being. Consequently, the being of Parmenides is continuous.

Zeno demonstrates indirectly the existence of a single, invariable and continuous being by showing that the hypothesis about the plurality, variability, and divisibility of being leads to contradictions.

Zeno's *aporias* are directed against the Pythagorean doctrine that space and time are composed of points.[17] Zeno indicates the contradictions in the supposition of plurality, by showing that plurality is infinitely small and infinitely great and, subsequently, that that which is faster remains behind that which is slower, that that which is in motion is at rest, etc.[18]

According to Zeno, one cannot suppose that the continuous, in other words, that which is infinitely divisible is the sum of indivisible elements, because on that supposition, the continuous would be, on the one hand, without magnitude and, on the other, infinitely great. Plurality is without magnitude because it is composed of indivisible units without magnitude; consequently, the sum of units must also be without magnitude. Plurality is also infinitely great because the units of which it is composed have a magnitude, for without magnitude they could not exist and would be nothingness. If these parts, indeed, represent plurality, they must be separated from one another, that is to say, between two parts there has to exist a third part which separates them, and so on, *ad infinitum.* In this case, things are composed of an infinite number of parts, and because of the magnitude of their parts which are infinite in number, they themselves must be infinitely great. Plurality, therefore, cannot exist, because it contains contradictory qualities.[19]

By a similar procedure, Zeno shows that plurality in number must be limited as well as unlimited. "If there is plurality, it is necessary that there be as many pluralities as there are, neither

---

[17]Cantor is of the opinion that the atomists were opponents of Zeno, while Tannery and Milhaud attribute this role to the Pythagoreans. The second hypothesis seems more probable.

[18]According to the testimony of Plato, Zeno knew how to present to his listeners one and the same thing, as being similar and dissimilar, single and multiple, in motion and at rest. Cf. Phaedr. 261 D.

[19]*Simpl. Phys.* 140, 34; 139, 5; 140, 27.

more, nor less. Being as many as they are, they will be limited. If there is plurality, pluralities are unlimited; because there are always units between units, and still others between the preceding ones. Thus, being will be unlimited."[20] This argument of Zeno means that if one supposes bodies composed of points, one must also suppose that the number of points contained in them is finite; it is, however, certain that other points exist between two points, however close they may be, if they do not coincide.

In the same way, space as the substratum of plurality is impossible, because the supposition of space entails a *regressus in infinitum*. If space is, it will be in something; for whatever is, is in something; and that which is in something is also in a space. Therefore, space will be in a space, and so on *ad infinitum*. Therefore, space is not.[21]

Concerning Zeno's arguments against motion, we shall say, without presenting them, that we agree with Tannery when he says that Zeno did not, by any means, wish to deny motion, but to demonstrate that it is irreconcilable with the conception of space as a sum of points.[22]

The argumentation of Zeno brilliantly achieved its aim: it succeeded in bringing about the rejection of the conception of empty space and of the monads of the Pythagoreans.[23]

Zeno's arguments against motion gave birth to two conceptions

---

[20]Cf. *Simpl. Phys.* 30 b, o.

[21]Cf. *Simpl. Phys.* 130 b. See also *Arist. Phys.* IV, 1. 209 a. 23. and *Arist. Phys.* IV, 3. 210 b. 22.

[22]"The aim of the Discourses he had written was very clearly defined by Plato, to whom one should evidently adhere on this: Zeno combatted the belief in plurality as a hypothesis and by demonstrating that, if this hypothesis is admitted, one arrives necessarily at contradictions, since one is equally driven to affirm that things are infinitely small and infinitely large, at rest and in motion. Thus, it should be well understood (and it is all too often left unmentioned) that, whatever his celebrated arguments, Zeno by no means negated movement (he is not a skeptic), but affirmed only its incompatibility with the belief in plurality" (*Op. cit.*, p. 248).

[23]Milhaud, a great partisan of the theory of continuity, glorifies these deductions of Zeno's and concludes that they are of an incalculable significance for science. "Science was going to be able to benefit from this dialectic related to such important ideas as the continuity of space and time. To bring about the triumph of like ideas, was almost to give life to mathematics all over again; it was to upset and remove the pitfalls which its own creator, Pythagoras, built against it with his conception of discontinuous plurality," etc. (*Op. cit.*, p. 138).

of space (and time) in both finitism and infinitism. Therein lies
their principal merit, and that is why they are interesting to us.
According to the first conception, space and time are composed
of indivisible parts, they are discontinuous; according to the
second, they are divisible to infinity, that is to say, they are
continuous.

Anaxagoras, with his philosophy, also contributed to the
establishment of the notion of the continuous in Greek
philosophy.[24]

According to Anaxagoras, matter is divisible to infinity, more
exactly, each part of matter is divisible to infinity. In matter, the
irreducible minimum does not exist; matter is composed neither
of the indivisible monads of the Pythagoreans, nor of the
indivisible atoms of the atomists, but is continuous, as conceived
by the Eleatics. The elements are infinite in number; the quantity
of each element is infinite. Matter is everywhere composed of
all the elements; the mixture of elements that occurs in large
parts of matter occurs also in the small parts of matter. Therefore, plurality in unity exists. "And as there is, in plurality,
equality of destiny for the great and for the small, it is possible,
in this manner, that there be all in everything. Nothing can be
isolated but all participates in all. Since there is no minimum,
it can never isolate itself and subsist by itself, but even now, as
in the beginning, all things are blended. There is plurality in
all, and, in both the greatest and the smallest, there is always an
equal plurality of distinct things."[25]

Consequently, the elements cannot be separated by infinite
division of matter. The diverse elements are not given in equal
quantities; the quantities of the elements in mixtures are diverse,
and this accounts for the formation of diverse bodies.

In the same way as the division of matter, the augmentation
of matter can also be pushed to infinity. "In relation to the small
there is no minimum, but always something smaller. For it is
not possible for being to cease to exist. Likewise, in relation to
the great, there is always something greater, and it is equal to

---

[24]". . . it is around the middle of the Vth century that one can regard
the concept of infinity as being not absolutely elucidated, but integrally
constituted. It is, then, such in Anaxagoras . . ." (Tannery, *Op. cit.*, p. 127).
[25]Cf. *Simpl. Phys.* 164, 25.

the small in plurality. Hence, each thing is in itself at once great and small."[26]

The elements of Anaxagoras differ, then, from the atoms not only qualitatively, but also in regard to their divisibility to infinity. Anaxagoras affirms, in opposition to the atomists, that empty space does not exist, that all is filled with matter.[27]

We shall mention also Anaxagoras' conception of the *nous* which, at a given moment, creates the world of change in producing rotational movement in the world of rest. The effect of the *nous* expands more and more and gradually organizes an increasing portion of inert matter. There is no limit that would mark the end of this action. In this conception of Anaxagoras, Tannery and Milhaud see the first use of the concept of infinity in the strictly mathematical sense.[28]

Anaxagoras interests us, however, as the founder of the first theory of the continuity of matter which is in complete opposition to the conception of discrete matter of Leucippus and Democritus.

Chronologically, the atomists are certainly the second forerunners of Bruno's doctrine of the minimum. In this doctrine, the influence of atomism can be recognized perfectly.

The atomists represent the reaction against the ideas of the Eleatics. The Eleatics denied the plurality of things and motion, because these two notions could not be conceived without empty space, and, in the opinion of the Eleatics, empty space is nonbeing. Leucippus recognized that movement is impossible without empty space, and that empty space is non-being, but he accepts it nevertheless in order to preserve becoming, i.e., appearance and disappearance, movement and plurality of things.

---

[26]Cf. *Simpl. Phys.* 164, 16.

[27]Cf. Lucret. *De Rerum Natura*, 1, vers. 843-844.

[28]"The world is a magnitude which grows indefinitely and can surpass every assignable limit as can a series of numbers. We recognize there a thought of a true geometer and can expect to find him just as rigorous and as distant from vulgar notions in cases involving no longer the infinitely great, but rather, the infinitely small" (Tannery, *Op. cit*), p. 282. "The universe of Anaxagoras is limitless in the precise sense in which a geometer would understand this. However far movement may extend, there will always remain more matter to set in motion and separate into distinct bodies, in a word, to organize. That is absolutely the concept of mathematical infinity in the sense of increase" (Milhaud, *Op. cit.*, p. 143).

According to the atomists, matter is composed of atoms.[29] The atoms are impenetrable, indivisible, full, continuous and extended. As one can see, Democritus multiplies the being of Parmenides without changing its essential qualities. It is by the supposition of empty space that Democritus multiplies the being of Parmenides. The plurality of things can only exist if being is separated by non-being or empty space.[30]

Among the atomists, empty space is taken in the absolute sense; it is nothingness which exists. Nothingness also exists, because being is no more real than non-being. Non-being exists, in order that being might be able to divide itself into a great number of parts.[31]

The atoms of Democritus are indivisible, but they are not simple, i.e., without parts. The atoms are indivisible inasmuch as they can never be separated into component parts. But they do have parts; they are not simple mathematical points. Although they possess parts, the atoms are so small that they cannot be perceived by the senses. Change in things is based upon the union and separation of atoms.

Consequently, everything is composed of atoms and empty space. The atoms do not exist independently of space; in order that phenomena may be explained, the full (the atoms) and the empty must necessarily penetrate one into the other, so that the empty breaks up the full, and that non-being breaks up being. This renders possible the diversity and the change of things.[32] In the atoms themselves, on the contrary, there is no empty space, for if empty space existed in the atoms, they would be dissoluble.

---

[29]"Democritus sees substances in the indivisible magnitudes." Cf. *Arist. Met.* VII, 13. 1039 a.

[30]See *Arist. Phys.* 1, 3. 187 a. 1.

[31]Aristotle says that Leucippus and his pupil Democritus put forth, as elements, the plenum and the void. They designated the first as being and the second as non-being. For that reason they asserted that being does not exist more than non-being and that empty space exists no less than do the bodies. These two elements (the plenum and the void) are the cause of the existence of matter. Cf. *Arist. Met.* I, 4. 985 b. 4.

[32]"In each part empty space is present in the same manner as the plenum. Empty space is non-being and the plenum is being." Cf. *Arist. Met.* IV, 5. 1009 a. 26.

Without the atom, magnitude would not even exist, for magnitude supposes the unit of magnitude. This argument is used by Democritus, who recalls Zeno's observations that division to infinity would leave no magnitude.

Atoms are qualitatively equal, but they differ in form, size, weight (which is proportional to the size), and, lastly, in their position in space. Bodies are composed of atoms; they are complexities of atoms. Qualitative differences of bodies reduce themselves to the quantitative differences of the atoms they contain. The atoms float, they are suspended in space, and, in virtue of their weight, they are forced to fall from high to low. Rendered possible by empty space, motion is the consequence of the weight of atoms and of their free fall in nature.[33] The movement of the atoms is eternal, as are the atoms themselves, whether one explains the movement in terms of the weight of the atoms, as Democritus has done, or adopts the view that movement is inherent in the atoms, as Epicurus will do later. The atoms collide continually, and this gives rise to whirlwinds which create innumerable worlds.

Let us also say that from fragment 155,[34] in which Democritus refutes the affirmation that the cone is composed of surfaces, Arnim[35] is fully entitled to deduce that Democritus denies *eo ipso* the very possibility of surfaces being composed of lines and of lines being composed of points, in other words, that he denies the possibility of geometrical figures being composed of indivisible parts.[36]

We shall not pursue the exposition of the doctrine of the atomists any further, because in its remaining part it has nothing in common with the doctrine of Bruno.

Plato was indubitably influenced by the Pythagoreans. He also seeks order and harmony in the relations of numbers. Inspired by the pythagorean doctrine, he sees harmony in

---

[33]Cf. *Arist. Phys.* IV, 6. 213 b. 4.

[34]Diels, *Op. cit.*, p. 412.

[35]*Epikurs Lehre vom Minimum*, pp. 7-8.

[36]Tannery arrives at the same conclusion. "It seems to me that he could have had only one goal, similar to Zeno's, namely, to establish that the surface of a cone cannot be regarded as a sum of circumferences" (*Op. cit.*, p. 261).

numbers, and, in the harmony, the condition of beauty. It goes without saying that for Plato, too, number is discrete. Yet, from the fact that Plato presents in the *Timaeus* the construction of bodies by means of elementary triangles, one can by no means deduce that he supposed the atoms as Aristotle believed he did, when he included Plato in his critique of the atomists.

Aristotle is a great adversary of atomism and, for this very reason, most unpalatable to Bruno. The arguments of Zeno against plurality and motion have influenced Aristotle to such an extent that it is by interpreting them that he has arrived at his conception of continuity.

Of Aristotle's numerous arguments against atomism and his numerous deductions of the continuity of space and matter we shall mention only that which relates directly to our subject, more exactly, that which provoked in Bruno assertions to the contrary.

Aristotle demonstrates in the following manner that indivisible magnitudes are impossible. That which is in the same place is *connected*. That which is in different places is *separated*. Things the extremities of which are connected *touch each other*. "*In between*" is that place where something which is changing appears before it has in its natural development attained its final end. A thing is *discrete* when it is bound to another thing in such a way that nothing of the same species exists between these two things. If what is in touch is discrete, then one calls it *that which is linked*.

That which is linked is *continuous,* if the limits of the composite parts which touch each other are the same.[37]

From this definition of the continuous it appears clearly that a continuous quantity cannot result from indivisible parts. For if the indivisible parts touch each other, they must touch each other either in their entirety or through their parts. In the first case they coincide and do not constitute the quantity; in the second, they would no longer be indivisible. Yet, if they did not touch each other, the continuous quantity could not result

---

[37]Cf. *Phys.* VI, 1. 231 b. See also Lasswitz, *Op. cit.,* p. 104.

from them. Consequently, the continuous can be divided, but it is not composed of indivisible parts.[38]

Aristotle, then, used in support of the continuity of space the antinomy discovered by Zeno. Through his identification of space and matter, Aristotle denies empty space. From this he deduces that matter is just as continuous as space. To refute the atomists, Aristotle imagined a mathematical atomism not established by Democritus. In brief, he identified the physical atom with the spatial point and thus discovered contradictions in the notion of the atom.[39] Aristotle's refutation of the conception of the atom is aimed in this manner against the mathematical atom as well.[40]

It is necessary to remark that *Epicurus* supposes the atoms composed of point-like minima. From the diverse dispositions of the minima result the diverse forms of the atoms. In this supposition of the minima in the atoms consists the difference between the conception of the atom of Epicurus and that of Democritus, who did not specify of what the atoms are composed.[41] Democritus holds to the position that physical bodies are composed of atoms that are not point-like, but are extended.[42] Epicurus adopts the opinion of Democritus that physical atoms are indivisible, but he considers them to be mathematically divisible.

Lastly, the Arab scholastics, known under the name of Mutakallimun, have been the forerunners of Bruno's doctrine of the minimum.

The Mutakallimun wanted to demonstrate the existence of God, by showing that the world is not eternal but was created by God. The atomistic theory struck them as the most convenient for their theological requirements; for this reason it was accepted by them. Hence, in order to demonstrate that the world does not

---

[38]*Phys.* VI, 1. 231 b. *De Coelo*, III, 8. 306 b.

[39]See Lasswitz, *Op. cit.*, p. 133.

[40]See *De Coelo*, III, 4. 303 a. 20.

[41]See Arnim, *Artic. cit.* pp. 5 and 12.

[42]See Zeller, *Die Philosophie der Griechen*, pp. 777-778. "Da nämlich die Atome nur deshalb unteilbar sind, weil kein Leeres in ihnen ist, so sind sie keine mathematischen Punkte, sondern Körper von einer gewissen Grösse . . ."

exist from eternity, but that God created it from nothingness, they analyzed space, matter and time into indivisible elements. To the Mutakallimun belongs the merit of having developed a purely metaphysical atomism to its ultimate logical implications.

Each body consists of very small parts, the atoms, which are not divisible any further. The atoms are simple substances, unmixed and without size; they are, therefore, point-like monads. An atom receives a certain quantitative value through its relation with other atoms. All atoms are equal. Bodies are formed by the composition of atoms and disappear through the decomposition of atoms. Therefore, all changes can be reduced to the aggregation, dispersion, movement and rest of atoms. The number of atoms is not determined and invariable, as ancient atomists believed them to be, but by his will God creates them and annihilates them. Between the atoms exists empty space, where there is absolutely nothing, neither body nor substance. Because one cannot imagine that bodies penetrate one another, empty space is used to support the movement of the atoms. However, it would be necessary to imagine such a penetration if all space were filled with atoms.

According to the Mutakallimun, time, also, is composed of discontinuous temporal instants, which are indivisible because of their short duration. This last idea is very characteristic of their viewpoint.

From the discontinuity of time they also deduced the discontinuity of motion. Differences between speeds of motion do not exist; one motion is slower than another because the intervals of rest in the one are greater than in the other. Hence, a moving body moves from one spatial point to another; between these passages exist intervals of rest, more or less great, which are the cause of the difference between the speeds of motion. From their atomistic conception of time and motion it appears that the Mutakallimun took into consideration Aristotle's remark on the relation between space, time and motion.

The Mutakallimun taught that substance can never be separated from its accidents. Each atom is inseparable from certain states, such as color, odor, movement and rest. Magnitude alone is not a state; it does not pertain to atoms but to bodies.

The atomism of the Mutakallimun illuminates the attacks of Aristotle against Democritus. Like the atomists, the Mutakallimun supposed empty space between atoms, but, unlike the atomists, who considered the atoms extended, they conceived of atoms as non-extended, i.e., point-like.

The Mutakallimun did not enter into the discussion of the concept of continuity, but founded their atomism on the opposition between reasoning and sense perception, explaining that the senses are incapable of perceiving the discontinuity of reality.

One objection made against the Mutakalimun was that their conception entails as a consequence the disappearance of the difference between commensurable and incommensurable quantities, between rational and irrational lines. Thus, for example, the side of the square, containing the same number of points as the diagonal, would be equal to the diagonal. Then the tenth book of Euclid, on the irrational quantities, would be superfluous. To avoid this objection, some of the Mutakallimun asserted that the square does not exist; others thought that we speak of the difference between the side and the diagonal of the square because of an illusion of the senses.[43]

Bruno, who was acquainted with all the doctrines of his predecessors, also knew, without a doubt, the doctrine of the Mutakallimun and was receptive to its influence.

Having thus terminated our exposition of the doctrines of Bruno's predecessors, we now proceed to the analysis of his work, *De Triplici Minimo*.

---

[43]See Lasswitz, *Op. cit.*, p. 134-150.

Chapter II

BRUNO'S DOCTRINE OF THE MINIMUM

De Triplici Minimo, a work devoted to the development of Bruno's teaching on the minimum, is metaphysical and geometrical. The metaphysical part is not separated from the geometrical; amidst expositions of metaphysical problems we encounter geometrical considerations; likewise, metaphysical reflections often interrupt geometrical explanations. This work shows all the superior features and all the shortcomings of Bruno's philosophy. In this work, Bruno demonstrates a great finesse of spirit, by discovering several truths which could have led to correct solutions of metaphysical problems if they had been developed to their ultimate consequences. Yet Bruno, absolutely unsuited for certain kinds of methodical exposition, presents them in a manner so fanciful and with so little system, that one loses sight of their importance, which remains hidden in his many unrigorous deductions. De Triplici Minimo is a tiresome melange of irregular hexameters (Bruno imitates Xenophanes, Parmenides, and, above all, Lucretius) and of *scolia* that are occasionally more poetic than the verses themselves. Bruno's style is endowed with a dramatic vivacity, but it is obscure, chaotic and surcharged with metaphors.

De Triplici Minimo consists of five books: (1) *On the Existence of the Minimum (De Minimi Existentia)*; (2) *Considerations starting from the Minimum (Contemplationes ex Minimo)*; (3) *Invention of the Minimum (Inventio Minimi)*; (4) *On the Principles of Measure and Figure (De Principiis Mensurae et Figurae)*, and (5) *On Measure (De Mensura)*.

The verses of the first chapter of the first book testify that Bruno sensed more intensively than all the other intellectuals of his time that soon there was to arise a new philosophy on foundations established by the ancient philosophers. Bruno sincerely believed that one can attain the truth in spite of the erroneous conceptions of false philosophers. "The spirit of *things subject to nature* produces each thing treating it according to its intrinsic [absolute] value, creates it according to a superior order and limits it by numbers. In the same way, the power of reason, as well as the living force of penetration of the human spirit, find the means for understanding these things and measures for their evaluation in this domain, from the boundaries of which the enormous crowd of sophists and ignorant men keep away, because they can thus appear more learned with less difficulty and effort . . . In this manner, they turn away from the admirable source of light, the origin of all that which beneficent nature paints in colors and enunciates in tones."[1]

After a highly poetic apotheosis to the sun (". . . Oh thou which hast revealed to mine eyes the infinite universe and the perfect worlds of brilliant stars"),[2] and a dedication to Prince Henry Jules, Bruno declares that in this work he will announce new truths, in spite of the difficulties that could be raised by "a certain half-scholar from among the deluge of grammarians,"[3] making use of ideas of his forerunners. "This is how old subjects can be used and how an ancient fable can embellish a new story."[4]

The *scolia* of the first chapter contain the general philosophical conceptions of Bruno: Here he gives the definitions of God, of nature and of reason. God is the spirit which is beyond everything. Nature is the spirit immanent in things. Reason is the spirit that penetrates all. God commands and orders. Nature executes and acts. Reason contemplates and examines. God is the monad, the source of all numbers, the element of all magnitude and the substance of everything composite, the

---

[1] p. 1, verses 1-13.
[2] p. 2, verses 30-32.
[3] "Sciolus quisquam e cataclysmo grammaticorum" (p. 5, verse 128).
[4] p. 7, verses 165-166.

excellence beyond all that is numberless and immense. Nature is the number that can be counted, the magnitude that can be measured, the moment that can be attained. Reason is the number that counts, the magnitude that measures, the moment that evaluates.[5]

Next, Bruno determines the relation among God, nature, and reason. God influences reason through nature; reason rises through nature to the knowledge of God. God is love, efficient cause, clarity, light. Nature is the loveable object, the fire and the ardor. Reason is that which loves, the subject; it is inflamed by nature and illuminated by God.[6]

According to these definitions, Bruno would be a theist, contrary to the general view that he is a pantheist.[7] Indeed, according to Bruno, God is the substance of everything; He is all in all, and all is He; He is the cause and the principle of all beings. Insofar as He is their cause, He is outside beings; insofar as He is their principle, He is immanent in beings.

Bruno proceeds then to the determination of the difference between perception by means of the senses and knowledge based on reason (*ratio*) and intellect (*intellectus*), a distinction to which he will return once again in this work and which he will relate to his doctrine of the minimum. Sense is an eye in a dark prison; it sees the colors and the surface of things as through bars and small openings. Reason sees, as through an open window, the light of knowledge that comes from the sun and is reflected towards the sun. Lastly, the intellect sees everything clearly from a great height; the intellect is the eye which sees beyond all particularity, all disorder, and all confusion in the universe and which contemplates the resplendent sun.[8] Knowledge based on reason is inferior to the knowledge of the intellect because reason is in direct contact with perceptions of the senses. But "reason would easily rise to intellect, if it

---

[5]Cf. Bruno's Latin text on p. 7.

[6]Cf. Latin text, p. 7.

[7]Ch. Bartholmess, *Jordano Bruno*, Paris, 1846, Vol. II, p. 388, thinks that in the works of Bruno there are as many pantheist-immanent conceptions of divinity as there are theist-transcendental ones.

[8]Cf. p. 7.

were not impeded by hesitation in the ocean of various passions."[9]
By contrast, in Bruno, the knowledge of the intellect corresponds
to the faculty of abstract concepts among the rationalists.

Bruno's naive reflections on man are related to the foregoing.
Man is a great state, formed by a curious diversity; in this state
are quantities of arts, classes, conditions, degrees, ranks, tissues,
instruments, functions and services. This is why it is possible
to direct this state toward a goal only in a final manner (but
that is the most worthy). And this happens whenever rationally
motivated will, director of all, is guided by some superior
principle. For the perfection of a man, like that of a state,
consists in the harmony of all the particular wills and the wise
will of the supreme master who has in view the good of the
whole.[10]

Bruno indicates here the method of his research, in expressing the idea (as in Descartes) of universal doubt as the point
of departure for philosophical reasoning. He who wants to
engage in philosophical studies must doubt everything, he must
not draw conclusions before taking into consideration two contrary opinions and before gathering the reasons for and against
and examining them well. Likewise, he must judge and conclude
about himself subjectively and about things objectively not
according to what is currently being said and told, or handed
down, or what the majority approves, or what has been believed
for a long time, or according to authority or reputation, but
according to the force of the examined doctrine and the truth
illuminated by the light of reason.[11]

Sayings and words, Bruno adds, can be used to express
wisdom and goodness as well as ignorance and injustice. Truth
and scholarship rejoice in the simplicity of the first two; laziness
and cunning rejoice in the ornament of the latter, and vanity,
with a mercenary solicitude, takes pride in their diversity.[12]

And in the end, Bruno (whose Latin works are distinguished

[9]"Ratio se facile in mentem attolleret, nisi variorum affectuum in oceano
fluctuans distraheretur." p. 7.

[10]Cf. pp. 7-8.

[11]Cf. p. 8.

[12]Cf. p. 8.

by a confusion beyond compare) categorically demands that philosophers be precise and brands confusion as the greatest sin. "And if any should try to exclude clarity and simplicity from this singular method of philosophy, may he be severely accused of parricide and sacrilege more so than if he had profaned the holy image of the gods."[13]

In the second chapter, Bruno proceeds to the exposition of his doctrine of the minimum, which, being an indivisible unity, is not only the element of all that which is composite, but also the principle and the seed of everything existent. He is conscious of having discovered a great truth; it is for that reason that he begins the chapter with highly inspired verses, saying that he has constructed a temple of hard diamond that will endure for centuries to come.[14]

The minimum is the substance of things,[15] their essence and their matter. Bruno admits that there exists a *triple minimum*: (1) *the general metaphysical minimum* or *the monad*, which means, first of all, unity as the basis of the entire existence, and, afterwards, unity as the basis of numbers (the minimum as the principle of quantity;[16] (2) *the physical minimum* or *the atom* (the minimum as the principle of the size of bodies);[17] and (3)

---

[13]Cf. p. 8.

[14]pp. 8-9, verses 1-5.

[15]"Minimum substantia rerum est" (p. 9, verse 5).

[16]"Minimum est . . . quantitatis principium" (p. 10). "The monad is present in the numbers rationally and in things essentially." (". . . Monas rationaliter in numeris, essentialiter in omnibus" (p. 10).) "Number is an accident of the monad, the monad is the essence of number." ("Numerus est accidens monadis, et monas est essentia numeri . . ." (p. 10).) "The monad is every number, because each number proceeds in its entirety from the monad, and the following number depends upon the monad . . ." ("Ut monas est omnis numerus; nam corpore toto emicat, et numerus succedens creditur illi" (p. 10, vers. 33-34).) "If you remove the minimum from everywhere, there will be nothing anywhere. Remove the monad from everywhere and there will be no number anywhere, there will be neither anything to count nor anyone to do the counting. Hence, under the name of monad one glorifies that which is the best, the greatest, the substance of substances, and the being through which beings exist" (p. 10).

[17]"Minimum est . . . corporearum vero magnitudinum . . . principium" (p. 10). "Composition takes place with the help of the atom and the atom is the essence of the composed." (". . . sic compositio accidit atomo, et atomus est essentia compositi" (p. 10).)

the geometrical minimum or *the point*.[18] In other words, the metaphysical minimum is, on the one hand, the monad as indivisible substance of the soul, and, on the other, the monad as unity; the physical minimum is the atom, and the geometrical minimum is the point. Therefore, each of these three minima is the principle of one speculative science: The monad is the principle of metaphysics, the atom that of physics and the point that of geometry. Bruno is satisfied with the explanation of each of the three kinds of his minima which we have just mentioned, and which are as general as they are fragmentary.

Bruno figuratively expresses that the minimum is the basis of all. "In this manner the minimum renews all, and if it did not exist as the basis of all, nothing would exist. If the monad did not exist, none of the numbers would exist, for the monad determines the species, determining each sort. This is why the monad is the first foundation of everything; the monad is God and nature which creates. The monad is explained by art as that which endures beyond each sort, and as that which is in each sort."[19] The minimum exists in a constant fashion in all, and is found beyond that which is enclosed by finite limits. It attains the infinite by creating, by linking, by renewing, and by eternally extending whatever is composite and whatever is simple.[20]

Hence, the minimum is matter or element, efficient cause, end and totality.[21] Whatever is the largest proceeds from the minimum, is contained in the minimum, formed in conformity with the minimum, and preserved by means of this minimum.[22] Hence, the largest is nothing other than the smallest.[23] Nature and art, which follows nature, compose by means of the minimum

---

[18]"The minimum is a point in the magnitude of one and of two dimensions." ("Est . . . punctum in magnitudine unius et duarum dimensionum" (p. 10).) "For him who observes bodies, the substance of the bodies is the smallest body or atom and for the one who observes the line and the surface, their substance is the minimum which is a point" (p. 10).

[19]Cf. p. 9, vers. 11-17.

[20]Cf. p. 9, vers. 18-22.

[21]"Est, inquam, materia seu elementum, efficiens, finis et totum . . ." (p. 10).

[22]". . . quia maxima quaeque Ex minimo, in minimo, ad minimum sunt, per minimumque" (p. 9, vers. 22-23).

[23]"Inde maximum nihil est aliud quam minimum" (p. 10).

and decompose into the minimum that which is composed.[24] The substance of things does not change; it is immortal; no power created it and none can destroy it, cause it to deteriorate, diminish it or augment it; whatever is created proceeds from the substance, and whatever disappears returns diminished to the substance.[25]

It is not necessary that there exist numerous kinds and forms of minima in order that things might be created from them, just as there do not exist numerous kinds and forms of letters and yet one can compose innumerable words from them. Bruno mentions here that, according to the atomists (Leucippus and Democritus), there is a difference between empty space and atoms and adds that there is only one form of atoms (of minima), the spherical atoms of which everything is composed. Empty space with atoms does not suffice for Bruno; matter by means of which they are about to unite is also necessary.[26]

Therefore, according to Bruno, the minimum is the basis of all; an immense plurality of things results from innumerable combinations of the minima. In the minimum is spirit (God) which penetrates into all things of the universe; for that reason, the minimum is at the same time the essence of things, the source of activity and the center of energy.

In our opinion, the difference between the monad and the atom in Bruno is purely nominal; in reality, the atom does not differ in anything from the monad. The atom of Bruno is not that of the materialists; it is the indivisible substance of the soul, as much as the monad is.

From what has been said above about the minimum, Bruno derives his doctrine of the immortality of the soul. Death does not destroy the substance of the body, and still less the soul (*Ex proxime dictis concluditur mortem ad corporis substantiam non pertinere, multoque minus ad animam,* chapter 3). Pythagoras had hit upon the truth in saying that one should not fear

---

[24]Cf. p. 9, vers. 24-25. See also the following passage on p. 10. "The subject and object of nature and of art, the composition and decomposition through action and contemplation start from the minimum, consist in the minimum and can be reduced to the minimum."

[25]Cf. p. 10, vers. 35-40.

[26]Cf. p. 10.

death, but await transition, because the substance of things is indissoluble.[27] Forms change continually,[28], for example, man's body,[29] but the substance of the body does not change. The minimum as element of the body is not susceptible to annihilation; no force of nature will annihilate it, the flash of lightning will not strike it, and the cutting tongues of flame cannot damage it. Only the order, place and function of parts change constantly, but the simple substance of things remains absolutely immutable. Hence, true substance is not something already composed, but rather that which one composes and the ultimate stuff of the composed by means of which one constructs.[30] That which is composed not being substance but accident, death is the decomposition of the composed.

Having stated in this manner the indestructibility of the substance of the human body, Bruno deduces from this with ease the immortality of the soul. As the great circle enlarges itself from the center, so also the creative spirit, having drawn the atoms from all sides, and having poured itself into them, steers this totality, till years pass and the thread of life breaks. Then the creative spirit returns to the center (the heart), and from there, renewed, penetrates the wide world, but we are in the habit of saying that this is death because we are headed toward an unfamiliar light.[31] Birth is therefore the enlargement

---

[27]"Oh, senseless man, if thou art afraid of the threats of death and destiny, thou wilt have reason no more. The words of the father from Samos have not been understood; this is why tales told by imbecils make thee tremble, and day-dreams of the crowd fill thee with a fatal fear, as though thou wert really made of corporeal parts alone" (p. 11, verses 1-5). Cf. p. 13.

[28]"Only the external forms change and perish, for they are not things, but are over things; they are not substances but accidents and determinations of substances" (*De la Causa Principio e Uno*, The Wagner edition, p. 242).

[29]"Does matter not change rapidly at different times, and, in its motion through continuous change, does it not incessantly take new parts while abandoning the preceding ones? And is the matter of thy body, in its parts and its totality, the same just now as it was before? Do the same blood, the same flesh and the same bones of the child remain in the young man? And is not all of this different again in the adult" (p. 11, verses 6-13).

[30]See p. 11-12, vers. 23-31.

[31]See p. 11, vers. 38-44. Cf. the following passage on p. 13: "We are what we are only by virtue of the indivisible spiritual substance around which atoms are gathered and clustered as around a center. Through birth and development the creative spirit expands into the mass of which we consist by diffusing itself

of the center, life the maintenance of the sphere and death the withdrawal to the center.[32] Our existence is therefore conditioned upon the indivisible substance of the soul, around which, as center, the atoms are arranged and combined.

The argument which decides in favor of our immortality is deduced from the following principle: The individual substance which constructs, amasses, arranges, vivifies and moves, and is as a marvelous creator of all this work, cannot be lower in rank than the bodies amassed, assembled, arranged and moved.[33]

"But only a few are able to have a clear presentiment that our life is death, and that to die sometimes means to rise to real life; for not all rise beyond this body; a great number sink into deep darkness, bending under their own weight and deprived of the divine flame,"[34] says Bruno under the influence of the Pythagoreans.

To his doctrine of the immortality of the soul Bruno ties the exposition of the doctrine of metempsychosis, established by the Pythagoreans and the neo-Platonists. Imitating also Heraclitus, Bruno claims that the changes in the abode of the soul are not fortuitous as the changes of the parts which compose corporeal masses are fortuitous. This is why certain souls pass through human bodies; of others it is believed that they go from these to the bodies of heroes; and the third group descends into the bodies of lower beings.[35]

The next thesis of Bruno is that everything turns in a circular line and imitates the circle (*"Omnia quodammodo circuire et*

---

[32]"Nativitas ergo est expansio centri, vita consistentia sphaerae, mors contractio in centrum" (p. 13). See *Articuli adversus Mathematicos*, pp. 24-25. "From the physical point of view, birth is a development of the minimum, or the expansion of the center to the circumference; death is the return of the circumference to the center. From the mathematical point of view, birth is constitution or presentation, and death, destruction or self-concealment."

[33]See p. 13.

[34]See p. 12, vers. 44-49.

[35]See p. 13.

---

from the heart to which its intermingled threads return like arrows. In this fashion the spirit returns by the same road down which it came and exits through the same door through which it entered." See also *De la Causa, Principio e Uno*, p. 237.

circulum imitari").[36] This thesis is the consequence of the affirmation, expressed in *De l'Infinito, Universo e Mondi*, that the center of the universe is everywhere, and its circumference nowhere. According to Bruno, all forces of nature and all bodies have the form of the sphere, and the sphere has that of the circle and of its center. The circle is nothing other than the visible center, and the infinite sphere is nothing other than the center which is everywhere.[37] In other words, all the forces of nature, however great they may be, can be reduced to the minimum, and are to be explained by the minimum,[38] because the minimum is distinguished by a marvelous force and grows into a great mass by composition.[39] At this point, Bruno speaks

---

[36]In *Art. adv. Math.* this is formulated very clearly: "All the works of nature are circle-like, and all motion, of whatever kind it may be, as well as the motion of elements, if natural, is circular. Rectilinear movement is the movement of that which is not considered as natural, namely, of parts, of that which hinders, escapes and withdraws. To walk, to swim, to fly, to grow, to feel, to comprehend, to endow with life, to live, to die is circle" (p. 60). In *De l'Infinito, Universo e Mondi*, Bruno explains in greater detail how he conceives of this circle. "As for movement, whatever moves in a natural manner, either around its center or around any other center, possesses circular movement. By that, I do not mean that this circle has to be regular in the strictly geometrical sense, but that it is regular according to the rule by which we see that the bodies of nature physically change their place" (p. 53).

Although a passionate partisan of the Copernican theory, Bruno takes the gravitation of bodies for an absurd hypothesis; in his opinion, all movement is circular. See Hallam, *Histoire de la littérature en Europe*, translated by A. Borghers, Paris, 1839, p. 108.

[37]See footnote 1 on p. 35 of the French original.

[38]See *Art. adv. Math.*, p. 24. "The power of all bodies is in the sphere, the power of every sphere is in the circle, the power of every circle is in the center, the power of all that is visible is in the invisible. The minimum is by its quantity potentially the largest, just as the force of a whole fire can be reduced to that of a spark. Thus, therefore, the minimum, which is hidden to the eyes of all, even to the eyes of the sages, and, may be also to the eyes of the Gods, contains all power; for this reason, it is the greatest of all." "It has been noted with prudence that the whole power of the circle resides in the center; this is one of the special principles of miracles. The soul is the center, it is also a circle that moves by its own motion; and, inversely, the circle is the soul of all the substances, all the faculties and all the works" (*Ibid.*, p. 60). "The center is the substance, the reason and the essence of the circle, for the circumference and the surface between the center and the circumference are only a development of the center" (*Ibid.*, p. 61).

[39]Cf. p. 14, vers. 10-11.

of God as the monad of monads which contains in itself plurality and magnitude, renews all and gives beings existence. God is entire, infinite, true, total, good, single.[40] Philosophers do not put forth the simple number and the single and self-same being as that which is true, unique, eternal, simple, same; therefore, they give it contrary names such as: principle, purpose, middle, end, nothingness, all.[41] Hence the minimum is the most powerful, because it contains in itself all movement, all number, all magnitude and all force. It pertains to it to compose, to enlarge, to form, and also to be composed, to be formed, and to enlarge itself to that which is the largest (according to Bruno, the smallest coincides with the largest).[42] Just as the monad causes all to be one, so also it causes all to exist; because of this, that which is not one is nothing.[43]

After these general determinations of the minimum, Bruno speaks of the disappearance of all oppositions in the minimum and in the maximum. In the smallest, the simple, the monad, all oppositions vanish; there, even and odd, much and little, finite and infinite are the same thing; thus, the smallest is also the largest and all that which is between them. This is seen first in God, of whom it is said that He is everywhere and that He is nowhere, that He is the basis of everything and that He governs all things. He is in all, but is not enclosed; He is beyond all, but is not excluded. He regulates all excellently and wisely; He is the principle from which all things flow, the end which terminates all, the mid-point which unites and separates all, the center which is everywhere, the innermost of the innermost. He is never extreme, because He measures and limits all, and He Himself is infinite and unlimited; all is in Him, and He is in nothing, not even in Himself, because He is indivisible and simplicity itself.[44]

This identification of the smallest and the largest in God is particularly characteristic of Bruno's pantheism. In this fashion, Bruno pantheistically identifies God and the minimum as monad,

---

[40]Cf. p. 14, vers. 16-19.
[41]Cf. p. 14, vers. 25-28.
[42]Cf. p. 16.
[43]Cf. p. 17.
[44]Cf. p. 17.

that is to say, as the indivisible and spiritual substance. In sum, at several places in his works, Bruno says that God is the one and the all (*en kai pan* of Xenophanes). Only, he did not specify here the relation of the monads with the Monad of Monads, God.

Because Bruno supposes an infinite universe, he claims that in the universe dimensions of length, width and depth do not differ and that every point is center. On the terrestrial globe or in the world there does not exist, starting from the center, any difference between the dimensions. In the diurnal rotation of the earth there exists everywhere a point east, west, south and every other point of this kind in relation to the whole surface of the earth. In the circle which is the limit or circumference one cannot subjectively distinguish that which is concave from that which is convex.[45]

The smallest and the largest angles coincide with the straight line; in other words, the sharpest angle and the most obtuse angle can be transformed into a straight line, just as they result from it by the rotation of the straight line CD around point C.

Between the smallest arc and the smallest chord there is no

---

[45]"In the minimum, which is the limit, the opposites coincide and are subjectively the same because convexity does not exist in the circumference and cannot be imagined otherwise than as occurring within the confines of concavity and together with it. Because you cannot draw this concavity independently of this convexity so that, if, for a similar reason, you should wish to take the trouble of calling things by their names, you will say convex-concave and concave-convex, just as in the case of the largest, where the infinite straight line necessarily becomes a circle, and the infinite circle necessarily becomes a straight line, I shall say circular-straight and straight-circular. Therefore, that which one does not really distinguish as essence within the composed, within that which is perceived by the senses, within the discrete, separate, extended, divisible, within that which is the simplest, within that which is principal, constant, same, eternal, true, within being, *is* one and the same; thus, truth itself is the beginning and the end, birth and completion, the alpha and the omega, or, rather, the alpha-omega. The following sentence of Xenophanes and Parmenides was therefore not false, but was simply too profound for the Peripatetics with their banal spirit to be able to grasp: being is one, immobile; it is that which is the same; it is the principle and the origin; as outside the unit nothing is essentially number, that which is not one, is nothing; therefore, being is one, truth is one, and plurality remains as accident, as vanity, as nonbeing: thus comprehendest thou when thou hearest the voice of the monad: *I am that which exists*" (*Art. adv. Math.*, pp. 25-26). Bruno concludes here upon the unity of being in the sense of the Eleatics, and upon the identity of the monad with being.

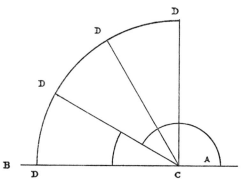

difference, just as there is none between the largest arc and the largest chord; the larger arcs CD, EF, and GH are, the more they approach the straight line; hence, the arc of the largest circle coincides with the straight line IK.[46]

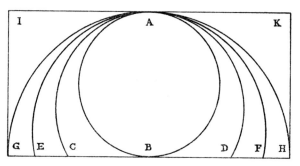

From this it follows that the infinite circle and the infinite straight line, as well as the diameter, the center and all the rest in the infinite do not differ in anything, just as they do not differ in the point which is the smallest circle. The greatest and most rapid movement and the slowest movement, that is to say, rest, are identical. For the point which moves along a circular line is at the same instant in all the points of the circle; therefore it is immobile. As a result, it is said of the divine wisdom, which reaches all and is in all, that it is the most mobile, because it remains in all, and that it is the most immobile because it passes the most rapidly from one end to the other. Motion is attributed to it, because it is mobility and life and because everything

---

[46]"The center, the smallest arc and the smallest chord are the same and equal, just as the greatest circumference and the greatest diameter, the greatest arc and the greatest chord are the same and equal" (*Art. adv. Math.*, p. 11). "The smallest arc and the smallest chord, like the greatest arc and the greatest chord, do not differ" (*Ibid.*, p. 27).

moves by means of it; rest is attributed to it because it is the eternity and the substance in and by which all exists and subsists.[47]

Bruno's deductions concerning the coincidence of the smallest and largest angle, of the smallest straight line and the smallest arc, of the largest straight line and the largest arc, and, lastly, of the center, the circumference, the arc, the chord and the diameter in the smallest and in the largest circle should be considered mathematical analogies, of which Bruno makes use to explain his assertions about the disappearance of all oppositions in the minimum and in the infinite, and in no way as special geometrical statements.

The line is, therefore, not anything other than the movement of the point; the surface is the line which moves; and the solid is the surface which moves. According to this, the point which moves is the substance of all, while the immobile point is the totality. This is valid for the atom and, above and first of all, for the monad; therefore, the minimum or the monad is all; it is that which is the largest and the totality.[48]

If observation follows the traces of nature, observation must start from the minimum, must consist in the examination of the minimum and must stop at the observation of the minimum.[49] From what has been said above, Bruno deduces that the observation of the minimum is necessary especially for the foundation of the natural sciences, mathematics and metaphysics.[50] "Without

---

[47]Cf. Latin text on pp. 17-18. On this subject, see also *Art. adv. Math.*, p. 27. "Hence, the physicist comprehends that the greatest or most rapid movement, than which there is none more rapid, does not differ from perfect rest. Hence, wisdom is that which is the most mobile, because it is immobile, and it is immobile because it is that which is the most mobile, and the prophets represent it in the two cited manners."

Bruno supposes two principles of motion. The first one, which is finite, corresponds to the faculty of the finite subject moving in finite time; the second, which is infinite, corresponds to the faculty of divinity which is, in its entirety, present in all, and moves in an instant. For the earth, as for all the other bodies in the universe, the two principles are valid. Bodies moved by infinite force are not in motion, instantaneous movement and rest being identical (*De l'Infinito, Universo e Mondi*, pp. 29-30).

[48]Cf. p. 18.
[49]Cf. p. 18.
[50]Cf. p. 20.

this principle can work neither the physicist, nor he who engages in the study of mathematics, nor he who studies the sublime truths of philosophy."[51] So Bruno reduces, then, all knowledge of nature to the knowledge of the minimum. Nature which creates things starts from the minimum; intelligence which learns these things must equally start from the minimum.

In order to prepare the minds for the comprehension of truth, Bruno begins with the destruction of the basis of falsehood,[52] and refutes first of all the proofs as to the infinite divisibility of space.

According to vulgar opinion, if one decomposes a quantity into however great a number of parts, one cannot in any manner arrive at parts that would be without parts.[53] The followers of the infinite, dividing matter and number, believe that they can never arrive at the last part; actually, going from number to number and from one part of the matter to another, they do encounter, without a doubt, the monad and the atom. "An unworthy illusion embroils the wretched spirit when it holds that the entire continuum can be divided by infinitely counting the parts; such a spirit does not see that number is added infinitely many times, and that this is no longer valid when quantity is subtracted from quantity."[54] If one supposes matter finite, then for the very reason that the largest part exists, the smallest part also exists; this latter is to be found in the totality, always and everywhere.[55] One can seek the third part of a whole, or the one-hundredth of that part, etc.; if one continues the division, one will arrive at the smallest part, and it will always come back, throughout the whole duration of the division.[56] It should be established that finite matter is not composed of infinite parts. When one adds parts to finite matter, one can pass on to infinity, just as when one adds plurality to finite number. By contrast, through subtraction and division of a finite magnitude one arrives necessarily at the minimum, just as through subtraction

---

[51]Cf. p. 16, vers. 79-82.
[52]Cf. p. 20.
[53]Cf. p. 20, vers. 1-3. Cf. p. 22.
[54]Cf. pp. 20-21, vers. 16-20.
[55]Cf. p. 20, vers. 41-43.
[56]Cf. p. 22, vers. 53-55.

of finite numbers one arrives necessarily at the monad.[57] Bruno's aim is to establish not merely that by division of matter one arrives at the last part, but that the last and indivisible part exists *before* the division.

Bruno interrupts for a moment his critique of division to infinity, to formulate his thesis about time. Time is absolutely infinite in the direction of the past as well as in the direction of the future. Therefore, time is infinite at every instant of duration, and every instant of duration is a beginning without end and an end without beginning.[58] Bruno figuratively expresses that time is the infinite present in which one does not distinguish the beginning from the end;[59] indeed, according to him, time is composed of indivisible moments and each moment is the middle point between two infinities. The assertion that time is infinite is the consequence of the assertion, expressed in *De l'Infinito,* that the universe is infinite; in the universe the earth is not in the middle, any more than the moon, the sun and the planets are there. Bruno says that this consideration could not be approached by those not able to understand that the earth turns around its center.[60]

The origin and basis of all the errors in physics, as well as mathematics, is the division of the continuum to infinity,[61] in other words, ignorance of the minimum. Yet the minimum is everywhere and always, the maximum nowhere and never. But the minimum and the maximum can be approached one from the other, in order that we may learn through this that the maximum, also, is everywhere. The maximum consists in the minimum and the minimum in the maximum, just as the monad consists in the plurality and the plurality in the monad. Reason and nature can more easily separate the minimum from the maximum than the maximum from the minimum.[62] Bruno ends

---

[57]Cf. p. 22.

[58]Cf. p. 23.

[59]"Tota ergo duratio est infinitum instans idem principium et finis" (p. 23).

[60]Cf. p. 23.

[61]"Principium et fundamentum errorum omnium, tum in physica tum in mathesi, est resolutio continui in infinitum" (p. 23).

[62]Cf. p. 23. Bruno expresses the same thing in clear and concise formulation in *Art adv. Math.* "Ignorance of the minimum makes the geometers of this

this chapter with general affirmations: The infinite is the center which is everywhere; eternity is the present which endures always the same, but which has the appearance of changing in the succession and change of things; the infinite body is the atom, the infinite surface is the point; the infinite space is the location of the point or of the atom. When one conceives the atom, one conceives all, but when one conceives all, one has not conceived the atom. One says, therefore, that the atom is everywhere. Since space is infinite, one says that the center is everywhere and that the atom is all.[63]

In the seventh chapter, Bruno makes a subtle distinction between the smallest parts, *the minima,* and their limits, *the termini,* which separate the minima so that the minima cannot coincide. In this manner he pushes out of the way once and for all the objection of Aristotle that the line cannot be composed of indivisible points. According to Aristotle, the points, being without parts, are in touch entirely and therefore coincide. Consequently, the line cannot be composed of points. In opposition to Aristotle, Bruno states his famous counter-argument. We are about to give Bruno's naive argumentation, which represents,

---

[63]Cf. p. 23.

---

century geometers and the philosophers, philosophers. If the minimum does not remain, nothing is to remain. If one does not, in a certain manner, recognize the minimum, one cannot recognize any quantity. Just as the unit is the substance and the essence of every number, so also the minimum is the substance and essence of quantity, geometrical as well as physical. For this reason we admit that there exists a twofold minimum: one in the plane, which is a point, and the other in the body, which is an atom . . ." (pp. 21-22). "Except for the minimum and the atom, or the atom and the point, I understand that nothing really exists" (p. 23). "The minimum is, then, the prime matter and prime substance of things, because it contains the maximum in such a manner that every magnitude, whether physical or geometrical, originates from it, exists in it, with it, on it, by it and according to it" (p. 24). "Because of the minimum there is a maximum; because of the center, there is a circumference, if all must exist because of that from which it arises" (p .24). "Thus, therefore, as nothing exists, except for the monad, as there is no quantity, except for the atom and the point, so also, except for the relationship and definition of the minimum, there is no measure, no geometer, and, consequently, no philosophy" (p. 26). "As nature sets limits by separating, art must also set limits by the same process. And as the minimum endures absolutely, one conceives the minimum in itself through a certain manner of reasoning" (p. 27).

nevertheless, a capital discovery in the history of doctrines about discontinuous space (pp. 24-31).

Bruno gives arguments which show decisively that a quantity cannot be divided to infinity. When the reason for which the peripatetics and their successors introduce the infinite is exposed and refuted, it will follow that a finite quantity cannot be composed, either actually or potentially, of an infinite number of parts. *In Bruno's opinion, the peripatetics are mistaken in not making a differentiation between a terminus which is not a part and a minimum which is the first part.*[64] First of all, the affirmation that quantity is not composed of first parts is not right. The finite continuum cannot be infinitely divided, either actually or potentially; one is bound to stop at the smallest part, in which, potentially, there are no more parts. Nor should one believe in the active power of the nature which divides more than in the passive power of the nature or matter divided, and inversely. Likewise, it is erroneous to follow the imagination or the mathematical science which divide to infinity, for neither the order of things nor any artificial use corresponds to their infinite progression. Whence, the mathematicians, who admit the infinite with more precaution, always take it for something indeterminate or as something as large as wanted, and never as the infinite in the true sense. It is imprecisely said that quantity is not composed of parts or, if it is, that it is not composed of first parts; and this amounts to affirming that in nature which composes there is nothing primary from which magnitudes proceed, the same as in art. But we cannot imagine anything without the first part.[65]

---

[64]Cf. p. 28.

[65]The first of the theorems about the minimum (*Theoremata Minimi*) in *Art. adv. Mathematicos* is the following: "Neither the division of nature, nor the division of art goes to infinity (though this division may sometimes be indeterminate), but is necessarily limited by a certain limit" (p. 10). And then, in the third article, he says: "The geometer and the physicist who do not comprehend that the minimum and the maximum exist for the same reason, are necessarily everywhere inexact, because they measure everywhere without measure. Reason is wrong when it divides to infinity. For it is evident that it does not follow nature, and that it does not believe it possible to attain nature through division, or compare itself to nature or surpass it, but (if it does not want to delude itself), it knows that it is erring and dreaming fantastically outside nature" (pp. 22-23).

It may happen that what has, in one division, been taken for the first part will, in another, be treated as the last part; but one never acts before having admitted a part which is the smallest in relation to the work at hand. Hence, as the work of art is indeterminate, the minimum is also indeterminate. But since that work is not infinite, endless subordination, that is to say, division of the minimum into still smaller parts, is not necessary. It is not so in nature, because in all her finite species, the minimum and the maximum are determinate. "For what reason, in God's eternal name, could nature be in need of the infinite?"[66]

In every order of parts must there not be a first part? If the first part did not exist, could there be anything of the same order after it? How can one recognize preceding and following parts which are without the first part? How can you say that there are larger and smaller parts which do not have the smallest part? Is the relation of that which is the smallest to that which is the largest, the relation of the first part to the whole, not determined by nature, as is the relation of that which is larger to that which is smaller? And as that which is larger tends toward the largest, does not that which is smaller tend toward the smallest?[67] Some might say, Bruno continues, that what is once taken for the first part might later be taken for the ultimate or, in some other act of measuring, for the totality. But even if this fact is taken into consideration, it is impossible to justify the assertion about the existence of infinitely small parts by lowering the quantity of the finite to the infinite through division as number is raised to the infinite through multiplication; in vain will the quantity of the finite be potentially enclosed in the infinite, since one can in no way affirm that it is actually infinite.[68]

Bruno cites Aristotle's classical argument against the possibility of space being composed of indivisible points: If one minimum touches another minimum, each is entirely in contact with the other; more precisely, each coincides with the other, and this does not make either larger; for a minimum cannot be

---

[66]Cf. pp. 28-29.
[67]Cf. p. 29.
[68]Cf. p. 29.

outside another minimum in one part and also be connected with the other minimum in another part, because it would, then, have two parts: one by which the other minimum is touched and another by which it is enlarged. But then this would not be a minimum, because, if it were a minimum, it could not make larger another minimum. That which is true of one minimum is true also of all the others. Therefore, the whole is not made up of minima; therefore, by decomposition of parts one never attains the smallest part.[69]

Bruno presents now his celebrated counter-argument: Aristotle could draw such a conclusion only because he did not differentiate between the *minimum*, which is the smallest part, and the *terminus* (or limit), which is not a part, but through which the smallest parts are in touch with one another. Bruno describes the difference betweeen the minimum and the terminus in the following manner: The minimum is not in contact with another minimum, either entirely or through a part; but through its limit, it can be in contact with several other minima; just as body is not in contact with another body either entirely or through an entire part, being in contact either through its whole extremity or through a part of its extremity; and as in the plane surface, where surface is limited by surface, and in the line, where one part is limited by another, one part is not in contact with another either through itself or through a part of itself, but through its terminus. Therefore the terminus is that which has no parts but which, nevertheless, is not the smallest part. A minimum is not in contact with minima through one of its parts or through several of its parts, but through several termini. So, the smallest triangle is in contact with three similar and equal triangles, the square with four similar and equal squares, the circle with six similar and equal circles. The same applies to the atoms of bodies, some of which are necessarily in contact, through their extremities, with similar atoms of the bodies.[70] *The minima, not touching each other directly, and being separated by the*

[69]Cf. p. 29.
[70]Cf. p. 29.

termini, cannot coincide; Aristotle's objection is, therefore, no longer valid.[71]

Bruno proceeds to the analysis of the notion of terminus. One ought not to believe that there exists something still smaller than the minimum, i.e., one ought not to believe that that through which one minimum is in contact with another is smaller than the minimum. It is necessary to emphasize that there exists the genus of that which touches, which is to say the genus of part; and the genus of that through which contact takes place, which is to say, the genus of terminus. There exists no part smaller than the smallest part; there exists no terminus smaller than the smallest terminus which is in the smallest part; for larger parts touch each other through larger termini, and smaller parts through smaller termini. A sphere touches another sphere, not at the smallest point but, rather, the atom (which is the smallest sphere) of this sphere touches another atom through a terminus (which is the smallest in the genus of termini). Whatever its size, the sphere is in touch with another equal sphere through a part neither larger nor smaller than the part through which the smallest sphere touches another equal sphere. But one is not to deduce from this that one of these spheres touches the other simply through the smallest point, because the sphere would have to be, itself, the smallest, to be in contact merely through such a terminus.[72] It follows from this that larger spheres do not touch each other at only one point but at many points; they touch one another, therefore, in a circle.

Bruno thus describes the nature of the terminus: The terminus added to the terminus does not make the terminus larger; the terminus is not a part; if each terminus were in contact with another terminus, they would contact entirely (it would coincide with the preceding one); for this reason, the quantity is not

---

[71]According to Brucker, the minima of Bruno are different from those of Epicurus; they are round and touch each other by the termini. From this, Brucker concludes that it is more likely that Bruno took his doctrine from the Pythagoreans than from Epicurus (and Democritus). Cf. *Historia Philosophiae*, p. 37. It seems to us that the former as well as the latter have influenced Bruno, but the invention of the terminus originated with Bruno.

[72]Cf. p. 30.

increased by the termini, either by points which are termini, or by atoms, lines, surfaces which are termini. The ultimate part of the surface is the line, the ultimate part of the line is the point, and not the terminus. Consequently, it is necessary to define the minimum as the part which has no parts, and the terminus as that which has no parts and which is itself not a part but which is that through which extremity is in touch with extremity, or part with part, or whole with whole. Thus, there exist, according to different quantities, different kinds of termini: the terminus which links line to line; then, the terminus which links surface to surface, and, finally, the terminus which links body to body.[73]

The contact of termini does not exist; parts touch each other through the termini but the termini themselves are not in touch; they do not constitute quantity, but are that medium through which parts touch each other in forming the contiguum or the continuum.[74] But, says Bruno, it is erroneous to conclude from the fact that they are not parts, do not enlarge the parts and do not contribute to the composition and renewal of the parts, that the termini must be infinite. Where the parts are not infinite, either actually or potentially, the termini cannot be infinite either. Since the parts are finite, the termini cannot be infinite, especially inasmuch as a terminus is always common to two parts. Hence, in the body, as in the surface, there cannot be more termini than there are parts (minima).[75] Through this argumentation of Bruno's it becomes evident that the termini depend upon the minima: The minima are primary, the termini secondary. Among the termini which cannot be divided (but can be multiplied through the division of parts) there are not some that are smaller and some larger, but they are the limits

---

[73]Cf. p. 30.

[74]In the tenth chapter Bruno explains this very clearly: a point which is a minimum, added to another point which is a minimum, makes a whole that can be decomposed into two points. By contrast, a point which is a terminus or limit of a quantity never stands to another terminus as part to another part, but is that through which a part touches another part. Cf. Bruno's Latin text on p. 41.

[75]Cf. p. 30.

of the larger, the limits of the smaller, and the limits of that which is the smallest.[76]

In this chapter Bruno gives also his analysis of the infinite number. The attributes: equal, larger and smaller cannot be implied in the infinite. In the domain of infinity, the small part is equal to the large part; there, the half is equal to the whole.[77] One ought not to seek differences of measure in the immense or differences of limit in the infinite;[78] here the difference between even and odd does not exist.[79] The infinite number is not composed of twenty or ten or five monads, rather than of a thousand; just as in centuries past (if one supposes that the world has always existed) months and hours have not gone by and numerous days and nights have not passed any more times than winters, summers, autumns and springs.[80] Of one infinity is

----

[76]Cf. p. 31. In *Articuli* Bruno explains the terminus in this manner: "A point which is a terminus is not a quantity; it is neither smaller than a quantity, nor the smallest; by this we distinguish it from a point which is the smallest part. It agrees, however, with the smallest part in that neither has parts. The atom cannot be a terminus, unless the same atom is also the smallest part" (p. 22). "If one wants to speak correctly, one will never refer to points, lines and surfaces which are termini as minima. For, the assertion, that the smallest magnitude is that which has no parts, is contradictory, although it does not seem to be so" (p. 25). "One must not admit that there is either an infinite number of termini or an infinite number of parts; there are not so many parts because there are not so many termini, and there are not so many termini, because there are not so many parts. For the *termini* suppose the whole and the parts" (pp. 35-36).

[77]Cf. pp. 24-25, vers. 26-29.

[78]Cf. p. 26, vers. 68-69.

[79]Cf. p. 26, vers. 73.

[80]Cf. p. 26, vers. 74-80. The refutation in *De l'Infinito, Universo e Mondi* of Aristotle's two proofs that the infinite is not composed of equal parts (*De Coelo*, c. 7) has the same meaning: "He does not stand on a natural base when he subtracts one part or another from the infinite. For the infinite cannot have parts, unless one notes at once that every one of those parts is also infinite. It is pure folly to pretend that in the infinite one part is larger and another smaller, and that one has a greater relation to the totality and another a smaller one" (p. 45). Bruno admits that this is just as valid for infinite space as for infinite time (p. 46). The following passage, from the dialogue *De la Causa, Principio e Uno*, expresses still better that in infinity larger and smaller parts cannot exist: "In the immense space an inch does not differ from a foot, or a foot from a mile, for man does not approach immensity any sooner by miles than by feet. Because of this, immeasurable hours are not any greater than innumerable centuries, and immeasurable inches not a larger plurality than immeasurable miles. One does not come any closer to a relationship, comparison,

born the same thing as of another, for if one number can be less
infinite than another, that number should be considered finite.
Hence, if among all numbers one finds a finite number, whatever
its name, because of that finite number every other number will
be finite; likewise, if any number at all is larger than another,
it is not infinite.[81] Since the infinite number is not composed of
two equal parts and since it cannot be obtained by multiplication of a finite number, Bruno concludes that in the domain of
infinity parts cannot exist without one another,[82] contrary to the
domain of finite numbers where there are differences between
even and odd, simple and double, and between that which is
equal, that which is larger and that which is smaller.

To the adherent of the infinite number Bruno gives the
following advice: "Stop continually multiplying parts by infinite
numbers, and adding to a part innumerable parts, and adding
to these parts other innumerable parts. For you will never have
peace if you keep multiplying parts by other innumerable parts
an infinite number of times, and if you penetrate the meaning
of infinite numbers, oh, you ridiculous counter and wretched
surveyor working without any rule or order, *infinitiplier* without
principles and constantly mistaken wanderer'."[83] By this division
into parts, in turn always further divisible, does one not end up
with that which caused Aristotle, where he speaks of principles,
to reproach Anaxagoras, who expressed the opinion that in the
infinite there are infinitely many times infinitely many parts?
Thus, in the infinite number there will be many numbers infinitely many times infinite.[84]

---

[81]Cf. p. 26, vers. 81-86. Also Cf. p. 31.

[82]Cf. p. 31.

[83]Cf. pp. 27-28, vers. 112-120.

[84]Cf. p. 31. In his dialogue *De la Causa, Principio e Uno*, Bruno accepts the
opinion of Anaxagoras that all is present in all in the sense that spirit or soul
or universal form is present in all things, so that all can be produced by all
(p. 241).

---

equation and identity with infinity by virtue of being a man than one would
if one were an ant; and one would not have drawn any nearer to it if one
were a star than if one were a man; likewise, one would not be any closer
to it if one were the sun or the moon, than one is in being a man or an ant,
for none of this is distinguished in infinity" (p. 281). This passage expresses at
the same time Bruno's idea about the identity of spiritual substance in all living
beings.

But, says Bruno, the error of Aristotle is no less great when he imagines an infinite line between finite termini. For if line AB, limited by two finite termini, is composed of an infinite number of parts, whether one supposes them proportional or equal, one will be able to draw punctually around the line a spiral which is indubitably infinite, although it is between two finite termini. For the line is not shorter when laid out than when implicit.[85] After this, Bruno demonstrates that Zeno's argument against Achilles' movement is based upon the omission of the difference, first, between the minimum and the terminus; second, between the minimum of time and that of motion; and, finally, between the minimum of impulsive force and that of the shock and movement produced. A thing of a certain species cannot determine a thing of another species; this is why one has to determine the minima by their proper definitions. One measures the one by the other only mechanically and practically, because demonstration by means of the homogeneous is artificial, the measure not being of a different species from that which is measured. It should be said at once that this attempt of Bruno to resolve the difficulty of Zeno's argument against motion does not resolve it at all.

Consequently, one ought not to believe that time has no existence apart from movement but must enumerate as many kinds of time as kinds of movement. On account of the different nature of species and genera, one must multiply the difference of the minimum, for the minimum of one species corresponds to what is large in another species. The minimum of one genus is contained by what is large of another genus, and itself contains what is large of still another genus. This is why the enormous terrestrial globe is but a point if one considers the periphery which one can imagine in the fixed stars.[86]

In the ninth chapter (pp. 37-39) Bruno determines a very important difference between the minimum which can be perceived by the senses (*minimum sensibile*) and the minimum of nature (*minimum naturae*). To explain this difference better and show that the minimum of nature cannot be perceived by

---

[85]pp. 32 and 36. See also *Art. adv. Math.*, p. 35.
[86]Cf. pp. 32-37.

the senses, Bruno makes use of the comparison of Lucretius, cited already in the preceding chapter, as argument for the existence of the minimum.[87] Lucretius asserts that elementary particles (atoms) are below the threshold of our senses and cannot be perceived, and cites as an example that there are animals so small that their third part cannot be perceived.[88] "We see animals so small," says Bruno, repeating the words of Lucretius, "that their third part cannot be seen by any means. What size should one imagine their brain and abdomen to be? How large their eyes?"[89] No art can define the minimum of nature, which is much below the minimum that one can perceive by the senses.[90] The most perfect eyesight perceives that minimum which is capable of being perceived by the senses; otherwise it could not be so perceived.[91] The perceptible minimum must be composed of the minima of nature.[92] The minimum of taste, touch, etc., must have certain qualities through which each is related to the senses; these qualities can only arise from the composition of the minima and the particular sense to which each is related. The minima are not distinguished in their natural and original form. The minima of nature are all equal, and it is as a result of their addition that some can be perceived by the senses while others cannot be so perceived.[93]

A propos the affirmation that the minimum of nature cannot be perceived by the senses, Bruno expresses his judgment upon those who study perspective and upon physicists. If light, they say, were made up of points, it would be visible as such.[94] Bruno, however, asserts that neither senses nor reason can

---

[87]Cf. p. 34, vers. 74-78.

[88]Cf. *De Rerum Natura*, IV, vers. 116-121.

[89]Cf. p. 38, vers. 10-13. "Lucretius successfully demonstrated that the real minimum is far below the minimum which can be perceived by the senses, because nature divides quantity in an astonishing manner, more than an eye, however perfect it may be, can perceive this. Whatever is perceived by the senses indicates that this decomposition does take place in things" (*Art. adv. Math.*, p. 27).

[90]Cf. p. 38.

[91]Cf. p. 38.

[92]"Democritus and the Epicureans rightly say that the perceptible minimum is composed of several physical minima" (*Art. adv. Math.*, p. 24).

[93]Cf. p. 38.

[94]"Si lux, aiunt, esset punctalis, videretur vel esset visibilis . . ." (p. 39).

determine that light is made up of points. One does not see the pinpoint makeup of light, but the diffusion of the light.[95] In other words, pinpoint light is not visible in its point-like nature, but through diffusion.[96]

In the tenth chapter (pp. 39-42) Bruno affirms that the minimum in genus differs from the absolute minimum (*"Distinguitur minimum in genere a minimo absolute"*). The minimum is double: (1) simple or absolute and (2), by hypothesis, that minimum which is formed differently according to the difference in subjects and purposes.[97] The point is the minimum for the geometer, the letter for the grammarian, the simple discourse for the logician; from several discourses the orator composes the first part of his discourse; so the moulder, the painter, the geometer, each fashion different minima in accordance with different interests and different materials.[98] That which to one man is large and composite will be regarded by another as simple and the smallest. By the difference in contemplation or in method, it can be proved that Pythagoras admits monads and numbers as the first principle of things; Plato, atoms, lines and surfaces; Empedocles, four simple bodies; the physician, four humours; the surgeon or the anatomist, flesh, bones, muscles and cartilages; the painter, hair, cheeks, ears, fingers, eyes, etc. But the monad of the Pythagoreans is simpler than the monad somewhere situated (the atom); the matter of Plato's bodies is simpler than are the bodies of Empedocles, which have certain qualities; and the four bodies of Empedocles are simpler than the four bodies of the physician, which consist of simple complexities. On the scale of the knowable some commence by taking their first elements at the top, and others, at the bottom, of science.[99] By the following comparison Bruno indicates the

---

[95]Cf. p. 39.

[96] Cf. p. 39.

[97]"Minimum vero bifariam non sine causa accipimus; est quippe simpliciter et absolute minimum, quale unius generis esse oportet; est et hypothesi seu suppositione respectuque minimum, quod pro subiectorum et finis varietate varium constituitur" (p. 41). See *Art. adv. Math.*, p. 11. "The minimum is double: physical or simple, and mathematical or according to the measure of man (ad hominem); the former is one, the latter multiple."

[98]Cf. pp. 40-41, vers. 31-37.

[99]Cf. pp. 41-42.

variability of the minima: The earth is the minimum for the eighth sphere; the circle inscribed in a plane is the minimum for the earth; the point at the center is the minimum for the circle, and the apex in the center of the circle is the minimum for the point.[100]

In the eleventh chapter Bruno establishes that every genus has its appropriate minimum. More precisely, every genus, species, force, order, faculty, affection, sensible form, distance, time, moment, weight, voice, accent, reason and law, each have their proper minimum.[101] There are as many kinds of minima as there are kinds of things; there are the smallest terminus, the smallest plane, the smallest body, the smallest reason, the smallest science, the smallest number, etc.[102] Since whatever is composed of parts consists of elementary parts, it results that one divides one and the same quantity into equal and unequal parts not according to the nature of things but according to one's will.[103] Hence, that which is in itself composed of a determinate number of parts appears in different parts and in different order.[104]

This chapter also contains certain explanations about the nature of the terminus which are of high importance for Bruno's attempt at constructing a new geometry, according to which space is composed of points, and about which we shall speak more specifically in the conclusion. But these explanations show at the same time how indefinite and confused are the postulates of that geometry of Bruno's. Bruno says that between the minima there is always a terminus, the principle of one part and the limit of the other.[105] He explains his affirmation in the following manner: "Because minima can be joined, they can also be separated; they do not penetrate each other, they do not mix, they only touch each other; hence the body is nothing other than the minima themselves. Thus, everything can be decomposed except the minima, and the minima can be neither decomposed nor composed. If this is so, they touch each other through two

[100]Cf. p. 42.
[101]Cf. p. 42, vers. 4-7.
[102]Cf. p. 44.
[103]Cf. p. 44.
[104]Cf. p. 43, vers. 34-37.
[105]Cf. p. 43, vers. 38-39.

termini proper to them and not through one alone, for between two termini there is contact, and this is why Democritus affirms that between bodies there is empty space. And since the minima touch the minimum not through all the points but through a certain number of determinate points, it follows that between a touched sphere and several spheres touching it, there exist spaces pyramidal in form, as among six circles touching and one circle touched, there exist empty triangular spaces. Such is the empty space which Democritus and others have thought to be outside the worlds, among the stars . . ."[106] This passage contains, first of all, the affirmation that the minima are impenetrable, that they cannot be mixed, but can only be composed and decomposed; then, the rather unclear affirmation that the minima do not touch each other through a common terminus but through two termini; more precisely, that contact is effected through two termini; and, finally, that between the minima of surfaces exist empty interstices triangular in form, and between the minima of bodies, empty interstices pyramidal in form.[107] Bruno compares these interstices with the empty space occurring, according to Democritus, among the stars.[108]

Although, like Leucippus and Democritus, Bruno supposes empty space and atoms, his atomism differs basically from the materialist atomism of Leucippus and of Democritus, who regarded life and spirit as accidental products of certain compositions of atoms. The minimum of Bruno is the primordial force, the creative seed and the divine spark through which all things exist. He conceives his minimum dynamically.

Bruno proceeds to a more detailed explication of his assertion

---

[106]Cf. p. 44.

[107]See *Art. adv. Math.*, p. 22. "Around these minima, which are added to others and make up something composed, I admit, as empty space placed between full space, according to the opinion of ancient sages, the minima in the genus of empty space; namely, in the plane surface of triangles situated between the convexities of circles in mutual touch and, in the body of pyramids, between the convexities of spheres in mutual touch."

[108]In *De l'Infinito, Universo e Mondi* Bruno admits the existence of infinite ether in which are located innumerable bodies. These bodies are also composed of voids and plenums, because the ether not only surrounds them but also penetrates them and is present in each thing (p. 32).

that the typical form of the minimum of plane is the circle and that the form of the minimum of body is the sphere (chapter x, pp. 44-47). All figures differ from the circle by angles and all bodies differ likewise from the sphere.[109] Whatever has angles can be diminished; the smallest circular plane and the smallest circular body cannot be diminished; this is why Bruno attributes the circular form to his minima.[110]

On the basis of his affirmation in the preceding chapter, Bruno says that in the plane there exist two fundamental figures which are as much the smallest as they are the largest: the triangle and the circle. In the body also there exist two figures which correspond to these: the pyramid and the sphere. For in the plane there exist curvilinear triangles as interstices among circular minima which touch one another; likewise in bodies among spherically-shapped minima in mutual touch there are pyramids with curved planes as interstices.[111] According to this, every plane figure can be decomposed into triangles, and every body into pyramids, as elementary parts.[112] As one can see, Bruno conceives empty space between his minima, which is to say, between the smallest parts of matter.[113] In practice, however, the body and the plane are regarded as limited on all sides by straight lines; thus one supposes a minimum which has the same

---

[109]Cf. p. 46.

[110]Cf. p. 45, vers. 6-10. In *De Immenso et Innumerabilibus* Bruno thinks that the elementary parts of the universe tend towards an ever more perfectly circular form, because a form endowed with angles is imperfect. Every drop of water which separates itself from the mass of water becomes at once round. Likewise, parts of earth tend to become round. Cf. footnote 2 on p. 60 of the French original.

[111]Cf. p. 47.

[112]Cf. p. 46—Compare *Art. adv. Math.*, p. 22. "Therefore, the smallest figure is the circle, and the smallest body is the sphere simply and absolutely; in the second place come the pyramid and the triangle. The circle is also the largest plane, and the sphere is the largest body."

[113]From a passage in *Art. adv. Math.*, it follows that the minimum of empty space is smaller than the minimum of plenum. "One understands and feels that there exists in nature something smaller than the minimum, when one looks at various kinds of minima. Because a plane which is empty space is smaller than a plane which is plenum; this is also true of the smallest body (as empty space with three dimensions) (p. 24). The same thing is expressed in *De Triplici Minimo*, p. 46, verses 45-47.

form as the entire figure, because one does not perceive empty space between the minima.[114]

The thirteenth chapter contains a renewed demonstration that the minimum and the terminus are not of the same genus. (*"Minimum et terminus non sunt in eodem genere quanta"*). The terminus is not a quantity, it is the limit of quantity; hence a point of this kind has no dimension but is the principle of dimension; it is that from which a dimension starts. The minimum is the first dimension of length and width; it is that of which dimension is composed.[115]

Since the finite and the infinite are differences in quantity, it is not contrary to its principle that that which is large in a simple manner, like the universe, be infinite. Rather, it is contrary to this principle that it be finite. If this is so, one cannot admit that the universe has no form, but must consider it spherical in form, which alone befits the infinite. A finite spherical figure is distinguishable from the infinite spherical figure, because the equality of dimensions which the first possesses from one point, the second possesses from all the points. This is why the infinite is simple and full in itself, while the finite is that in relation to something. Only in the infinite is the center, which is the reason of the sphere, in every part. The terminus has no dimension. In the minimum, dimension cannot be distinguished originally. In the circle the two dimensions (length and width) cannot be distinguished actually. In the finite sphere, starting from the center, there is no difference among the three dimensions. In the infinite sphere the dimensions do not differ either taken up from any point or directed toward any point. Therefore, the largest and the smallest have the same form.[116]

---

[114]Cf. p. 46, vers. 47-52.

[115]Cf. p. 48, vers. 1-6. Also: "Terminus est principium dimensi ut unde seu de quo, minimum vero ut ex quo" (p. 49).

[116]Cf. p. 49. The following axioms concerning the sphere are in direct connection with these assertions: "In the sphere, the length, the width and the depth, the high and the low, the right and the left, and other differences of dimension are the same." "It is necessary, in the nature of things, for the sphere to be twofold, that is, finite as well as infinite. The infinite sphere, however, is more spherical than the finite sphere" (*Art. adv. Math.*, p. 14).

The following theorem, which is somewhat unclear, expresses the same thing: "It is rightly said that the spheric figure is the most spacious, but our

At the end of the chapter Bruno criticizes Aristotle who, according to him, had not been capable of understanding the depth of this assertion when he demonstrated, in opposition to Xenophanes, that the infinite excludes the definition of the sphere, that of every figure and even that of bodies.[117]

In the last chapter of the first book (chapter 14, pp. 49-53) Bruno proclaims that the minimum can be the subject of observation, though it cannot be perceived by the senses. The sense receives the certitude about the minimum from that which is large, for the minimum and the large are linked to one another by the fact that the minimum becomes large through composition.[118]

This chapter contains a very important consideration of Bruno's geometry: no figure can grow through the addition of one single minimum, but rather a definite number of minima is always necessary. An order of minima, whereby the surface of a figure increases without changing its form, Bruno designates by the name *gnomon*. The smallest circle, the circle of a single minimum, increases when one adds to it six more minima; thus, the circle larger than a minimum is composed of seven minima.[119] Bruno names the figure which represents a minimum in touch with six equal minima, *the plane of Democritus*.

On the figure one sees clearly that empty spaces between the minima form curvilinear triangles.[120] This figure also shows

---

[117]Cf. p. 49.

[118]Cf. p. 52.

[119]Cf. p. 50, vers. 8-14.

[120]In *Art. adv. Math.*, in the third theorem about the minimum, Bruno treats triangular spaces as minima. "A minimum is primarily, principally and simply a circle and then a curvilinear triangle" (p. 11).

---

popular philosophers do not understand that this is so, because by this figure one has to represent the infinite. Nevertheless, for those who take infinity into consideration, it is evident that the sphere is at the same time the least extensive of figures. Thus, this proposition (like many others) is taken by our antisages in a completely wrong sense; and yet, ancient sages took it in another sense" (*Ibid.*, p. 5). On page 22 one can read: "The greatest of the infinities is the spherical infinity, since the infinite is in itself a perfect sphere. The infinite surface is the most perfect circle, and the infinite body, which (as we believe) exists or is supposed to, is necessarily a sphere and receives the very definition of the sphere."

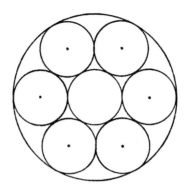

that the smallest triangle is composed of three minima,[121] and the smallest square of four minima. It is equally evident that the circle increases through the addition of 12, 18, 24, etc. minima.

Bruno attacks those who "foolishly treat the absurd doctrine of triangles and other parts of the sphere in the plane," because we cannot determine the number of spherical figures in a plane just as we cannot determine the number of planes in a spherical body.[122] The reason for the spherical triangle in a sphere is quite identical to the reason for the rectilinear triangle in a plane; accordingly, it is not worth the trouble to add anything to the principles of Euclid.[123] The elements of Euclid suffice to all; they contain perhaps somewhat more than is necessary; because of that, it would be preferable if they were more concise.[124] At this point, Bruno speaks favorably of Euclid, but complains about those who have had the audacity to profane ancient methods with new ones and who apply themselves to the proliferation of methods. "Multiplication of propositions and axioms is a sign not of a higher knowledge, but of a lack of greater capacity;

---

[121]Bruno imagines that the smallest triangle consists of circles and curvilinear triangles. The following quotations illuminate this conception of Bruno's: "Where one supposes all the plane figures to be composed of rectilinear triangles one has certainly conceived the continuum, but not the smallest continuum, or one composed of smallest parts, for we have shown that the rectilinear triangle is composed of a curvilinear triangle and a circle" (*Art. adv. Math.*, p. 23).

[122]Cf. p. 53.

[123]Cf. p. 53.

[124]Cf. p. 51, vers. 47-52.

of greater stupidity and ignorance, for an artist is the more perfect the fewer his instruments and means."[125]

In the first chapter of the second book (*Considerations Starting from the Minimum*) Bruno affirms that from the light of one truth (the truth about the minimum) flashes the light of many truths, just as one absurdity is followed by many others. (*Ex luce unius veritatis multiplicis veritatis lumen exsurgit, sicut uno ab absurdo plurima consequuntur.*") Here he presents how the minimum develops in the plurality of the world.

There exists a matter, a form, an efficient cause, the minimum. In each order, each gradation, each analogy one starts from the minimum; plurality consists in the minimum and returns to the minimum, which one has to regard as the first subject, the first example and the first agent. The minimum is potentially the largest, the large, the whole, similar to a spark which can expand into an enormous flame, if one gives it matter.[126] As among bodies some are inflamed very easily; others, with difficulty or great difficulty, so also among the senses, spirits and intellects of various men, some understand the truth about the minimum quickly, while the others cannot grasp it or do not want to understand it.[127] "Consequently, one man alone is the wisest (Bruno thinks of himself), the number of sages is restricted, the number of imbeciles is infinite."[128] The spirit that has understood the truth about the minimum and about the monad rises, in a determined order, to the large and to plurality and from there to the innumerable and the infinite, and returns afterwards the same way.[129]

In this book, the first geometrical consideration of importance is found in the second chapter (p. 56-57), where it is said that the perfect circle cannot be perceived by the senses (*"Circulum verum non esse sensibilem"*). The circle that can be perceived by the senses does not have all the points at an equal distance from the center, as required by the nature of the circle. For this reason, the circle that differs by a point is not the same

---

[125]Cf. p. 53.

[126]Cf. p. 55.

[127]Cf. p. 55.

[128]"Hinc vere sapientissimum est unum, quiddam sapientes pauci, stultorum vero infinitus est numerus" (p. 55).

[129]Cf. p. 55.

circle.[130] When the perfect circle presents itself to the senses, it is evident that the senses do not perceive it clearly, but dimly.[131] Just as the senses cannot perceive a point, so also they cannot perceive the perfect circular line.[132] For the peripatetics, one faculty perceives the circle, and the other judges about its reality and admits that it is perceptible. Contrary to what he expressed in the first chapter of the first book about sensory perception on the one hand and knowledge by reason and by intelligence on the other, Bruno now affirms that this other faculty, usually called the internal sense, does not have a special superiority over the first faculty, but that, in the final analysis, it can be reduced to the first faculty. Bruno calls that other faculty intelligence, in order to distinguish it from the first one.[133]

Bruno's next thesis is that the senses provide us with the first notion of the circle; to this end he gives an analysis of sensory perception, and demonstrates that the limits of that perception are strictly determined. "That which is perceived by the senses cannot rise to real understanding, just as sense cannot attain the true kind of intelligence. The faculty of the senses varies according to different senses; the ear does not perceive light and colors, the eyes do not perceive noise, cry and sound; the senses remain in the complexities of a single kind."[134]

Bruno teaches the relativity of sensory perception and consecrates to this doctrine a long and systematic exposé (pp. 58-61). ". . . What is agreeable to one ear is disagreeable to another; what seems excellent to one eye, is incompetent to another; the food that was pleasant when one was hungry becomes nauseous after the individual has been satiated; the thistle is agreeable to the taste of a jackass; to that of man it is too piquant; hemlock is the most agreeable nourishment to the goat, but it is pernicious

---

[130]Cf. p. 56, vers. 6-9. Cf. also the following: "Sensus verum circulum non apprehendit, qui uno de innumerabilibus exorbitante puncto non est ipse" (p. 56).
[131]Cf. p. 56.
[132]Cf. p. 56, vers. 13-14. "A perfect sphere cannot be perceived by the senses; it cannot be so perceived any more than can the atom of nature itself; moreover, for many reasons, it is even necessary that the sphere should be still less so" (*Art. adv. Math.*, p. 15). "A perfect circle cannot be perceived by the senses any more than can a simple atom" (*Ibid.*, p. 59).
[133]Cf. p. 56-57.
[134]Cf. p. 57, vers. 18-23.

to man . . . A monkey is very good-looking to another monkey; to man both monkeys are ridiculous. The melancholics see, in their mood, what others do not see. A patient cannot make a correct judgment about things that affect him painfully before he has compared this impression with the one which the same things produce upon him when he is well. In the opposite case, he judges things according to general opinion, like the congenitally blind who, not knowing that about which they speak, discuss colors according to what they have heard about them."[135]

In order that the truth might be expressed, it is necessary to correct the form of speech ". . . for those who speak prudently will not say: *this smells good, that tastes good, this sounds good, that looks beautiful, but will add: for me, now, at a certain time.*"[136] Therefore, nothing is good or bad, agreeable or disagreeable, beautiful or ugly in itself and absolutely, but the same objects receive different names according to the subjects to which they relate. That which is honest and shameful is not absolute, but varies with customs. Philosophy which teaches one how to abstract from the particular must define the useful and the good in itself differently from the useful and good in relation to human nature. Among the philosophers one should listen to those who are guided by the principle that in nature there is nothing absolutely good and absolutely true, but if something of that sort does exist one ought to seek it beyond and outside nature. One should listen as much to those who assert that whatever is said is true, even contradictions, as to those who think that nothing is true, because they do not rise in intelligence beyond the limit of nature and yet believe that there are oppositions in nature. Certain philosophers put everything according to their whim in the order of the good and true (following the assertion that there is nothing which is not good for someone), and affirm that no sense deceives; others, however, (following the assertion that there is nothing which is not bad for someone) think that everything should be reduced to the order of the false and unbecoming. In Bruno's opinion, those

---

[135]Cf. p. 58.

[136]". . . circumspectius enim loquentes non dicent *hoc bene olet, hoc bene sapit, bene sonat, pulchrum habet specimen,* sed addet *mihi, nunc, aliquando*" (p. 58).

who do not go beyond sensory perception should admit that nothing is absolute because that which weakens one provokes the birth of another; that which preserves one, destroys another; for different people different things are good or bad, joyous or sad, for some more, for others less, for some always, for others sometimes.[137]

Therefore, from the perspective of the object, good and evil, true and false are not determined; thus, from one point of view it can be said that all is good, from another, that all is evil, and, from yet a third point of view, that nothing is either good or evil or that all is sometimes evil and sometimes good. Consequently, differences between good and evil, sweet and bitter, useful and useless are quite relative. Those who see clearly will conclude with ease that there is no sense which deceives or is deceived, because each sense judges its objects according to its particular capacity, which is its proper, true and unique measure.[138] That which is perceived by the senses is true not in relation to a common and general measure but in relation to a measure which is homogeneous, particular and variable. To want to define universally that which is perceived by the senses amounts to the same thing as to want to define by means of the senses that which is intelligible. As far as the external senses are concerned, there may be different degrees of perfection and imperfection, but the senses are not capable of judgment about truth and falsehood. By means of the eye we see light, color and movement, but we cannot see the true with the eye, because the eye does not possess the capacity with which we distinguish true color and true light from illusions of the same kind. He who affirms that man is an animal should be acquainted with man and animal, and know that the nature of the animal can be re-encountered in man; and all other things, such as the milieu and the circumstances, are directly or indirectly necessary for that affirmation. The external senses can perceive only the simple kind of object; the internal faculty alone can pass from the color and figure of an object to its name, to its essence, to that which renders it different from other objects.[139]

---

[137]p. 58-59.
[138]Cf. p. 59-60.
[139]Cf. p. 60.

Bruno anticipates next the assertion of Locke: *"Nihil est in intellectu, quod antea non fuerit in sensu,"* by this affirmation: "there is nobody who would dare deny that a deaf person cannot imagine, and that he cannot hear in a dream, sounds he never heard, nor that a blind one can see colors and forms he never saw."[140]

From the cited ideas it would seem to follow that Bruno was an empiricist although in the first book he understood the knowledge of the intellect in the sense of the abstract concepts of the rationalists. In fact, he presented here the principles of the empiricist theory in so convincing a manner, that one could take him for the precursor of Locke and Hume. But, although we encounter in the works of Bruno ideas according to which the origin of our knowledge would be in experience, most of Bruno's assertions show that he was a rationalist. In brief, Bruno never undertook a systematic analysis of the origin of our knowledge; he did not especially occupy himself with problems of the theory of knowledge, not having enough logical need to formulate them clearly.

The fourth chapter (pp. 61-66) develops the thesis that a perfect circle is not possible in nature. Although in the infinite the opposites coincide, Bruno teaches, nevertheless, that the world of phenomena is characterized by individuation and diversity. All things in nature are undergoing perpetual change. "In the forest of creative nature we never find one part similar to another part, as atoms are similar to atoms, because elementary parts are endowed with that quality, if anything can be endowed with it."[141] Things in nature, some of them more and others less, some more slowly and others more quickly, change, rush, move and pursue one another continually.[142] Although it seems to the senses that a form remains the same for some time, this is impossible, according to the nature of things.[143] Bruno enlarges his previous affirmation that the perfect circle cannot be perceived by the senses: a circle composed of parts, all of which are equal and equidistant from the center, does not

---

[140]Cf. p. 61.
[141]Cf. p. 61, vers. 1-4.
[142]Cf. p. 65.
[143]Cf. p. 65.

exist in nature, and no art can create it.[144] In nature, there is nothing pure, like, similar or equal to itself or, for that matter, to something else, either in its entirety or in any of its parts.[145]

Bruno develops, with persuasion, his idea that all things in nature continually change in form and position. To those far from one another it seems that they have the same center; yet, each and every one of them has its own center.[146] If a pebble falls from a slope into a calm body of water, the waves form circles in a continuous order, so that it seems that this is one and the same circle enlarging itself; however, this is always a new circle, because new waves keep arriving without surcease. One believes that one obtains here a circle perfect from all sides, but that is inexact, because the form of the pebble that falls is not that of a perfect circle. No wind and no liquid are the same at two different instants. No part is equal to another part, although the incessant movement easily deceives the eyes. Voice and tone change, for a similar reason, according to the *milieu*, and their equal diffusion in all directions is not necessary. Nor does air expand in an even manner and by continuous movement. The waves of the sea move even when they appear calm.[147] Likewise light, heat, odor, do not travel in a continuous manner, in equal times, within one and the same space, at one and the same place, and with an equal force, although they do expand spherically, and though they do diminish and disappear in that same way.[148] The infinite alone is a perfect sphere, on all sides; and the minimum alone is the perfect circle, because there is nothing unequal in them.[149]

In this chapter one finds a digression in which Bruno refutes the peripatetics who, with the fifth essence, created the spheres, the worlds and the sky with its movements and its circles. Contrary to this, Bruno establishes ("we who are not accustomed to satisfying the hunger of the soul with the simple word that we understand but seek beyond the senses the bread of better

---

[144]Cf. p. 63, vers. 5-7.
[145]Cf. p. 62, vers. 34-85.
[146]Cf. p. 62-63, vers. 43-47.
[147]Cf. pp. 63-64, vers. 56-81.
[148]Cf. p. 64, vers. 93-100.
[149]Cf. p. 64, vers. 101-103, and p. 66.

and stronger reasons") that "the new heaven" (*caelum novum*) exists, namely, an immense space filled with ether (*unum immensum spacium aethereum*"), in which there are innumerable worlds of the same kind as our world. In this manner, "the new earth" (nova tellus) comes out of the dark; she is similar to the moon, to Venus and to Jupiter.[150]

After this, Bruno returns to his earlier thesis: whatever one sees with the eyes is composed of the same elements, and occurs in a continuous order of variability and vicissitude. Everything, except the atoms, results from composition; consequently, everything changes. By the flux of innumerable atoms bodies are incessantly modified in all their parts.[151] So, in composite bodies nothing is straight or circular in a simple manner, nothing is full in a simple manner, except the atoms, nor empty in a simple manner, except the space which is among three atoms in a plane and among four atoms in a body. Consequently, one must not consider anything to be simply continuous and unique other than the atoms, the universal space and the substance between and around bodies.[152] Nothing seems composed of more regularly distributed parts than the diamond; nothing seems more semicircular than the rainbow, nor more limited than the circle, nor more concave than the nocturnal horizon. Nevertheless, to those who examine more profoundly, the most evident inequality will appear, as much from the perspective of the object and of sense as from the perspective of the circumstances in all these things and all other things natural and artificial.[153] Bruno's throught is the following: atoms are invariable, but complexities of atoms, bodies, are subject to perpetual change, because the spirit of the world is in them. For this reason, matter constantly changes and no body remains identical.

From the fact that everything in nature changes, Bruno concludes that it is impossible to show in matter two completely equal figures or two completely equal lines, or to repeat a figure or a line. (*"Duas figuras vel lineas in materia omnino aequales*

---

[150]Cf. p. 65.
[161]Cf. p. 65.
[152]Cf. p. 66.
[153]*Ibid.*: "Nihil videtur . . ."

ostendere vel bis eandem repetere est impossibile," chapter 5, pp. 66-72.)[154]

According to Bruno, all is in continual flux: weight, milieu and subject change incessantly. One cannot find a man who would weigh the same on two different weighings.[155] The instruments with which we measure things deceive; the compass always measures different things.[156] Among the norms which determine things some are not less false than others. To take one norm instead of another means to carry the error from one place to another. There are no two weights, two lengths, two voices, or two harmonies that would be equal in all parts. Those who have said that movement is unequal have understood it exactly; in effect, movement is just as unequal to itself at two different moments, as it is to another movement.[157] One should not believe that the exact half has been found, because one has distinguished that which is smaller from that which is larger. Although it seems that numbers are formed in a simple manner, a certain kind of number is not equal to another kind.

Numbers not being equal, things in which there are several kinds of numbers, several forms and several differences in matter, time, milieu, efficient cause and movement, can still less be equal. One ordinarily considers ten trees to be equal to ten other trees, but that is false; for no tree is equal to another tree.[158] The measure and that which is measured are not identical; they differ as the logical thing differs from the physical.[159] Therefore, a certain compound cannot be identical to another compound. Since all is in process, nothing can be determined with precision. "The circle is not in contact through the same numbers by which

---

[154]"It is impossible to draw or find in nature two completely equal circles, or pass through the same circumference twice, and the impossibility is even more obvious when it comes to finding some other line or some other figure equal to another line or another figure. For that reason, Cusanus was right in saying that it is always possible to find a circle more perfect than another circle" (*Art. adv. Math.,* p. 60).

[155]Cf. p. 66, vers. 13-14.

[156]Cf. p. 67, vers. 27-30.

[157]Cf. p. 68, vers. 48-55.

[158]We find the same thought in Leibniz: "One will never find two leaves in a garden, or two drops of water perfectly alike" (*Opera Philos.,* ed. Erdmann, p. 765).

[159]Cf. pp. 68-69, vers. 66-80.

it was once touched, just as you will not find the same source twice; and as one cannot see the same flame of a torch twice, because you yourself are not the same,"[160] says Bruno in the sense of *panta rei* of Heraclitus. Fire does not remain numerically the same at two instants; it flickers more rapidly than can be observed by the senses.[161]

It is not possible to designate twice the central point of a line, the same as one cannot find two absolutely equal parts in the area of a circle, just as from the same point one cannot twice construct the same circle, and just as two apertures of the compass do not represent equal intervals.[162] Also, it is not possible to discover, in whatever species it may be, two individuals, two days, two circles or two years that would be equal or similar. All attempts at a precise determination of the length of a year are in vain.[163] Bruno cites an interesting example to illustrate the difference between mathematical quantities and those which appear in nature: if the length of two men or two plants were the same as that of two lines, one could, doubtless, find an instant, in the past, in the present or in the future, at which the length of the one would be equal to that of the other. For all men, at first short of stature, pass through the intermediate size and become adults; then, at some moment, all men should attain the same linear length. But that would be comparing a mathematical line to another line, and not comparing one man physically to another man, whose length is composed of innumerable lines which cannot be qualitatively and quantitatively equal to other innumerable lines.[164]

"Equality can be found in things which always remain the same (Bruno is thinking of the minima); things which change are unequal to themselves at two instants or to other things at every instant."[165] In spite of the equality of the original minima, different species suppose different minima; thus, one species becomes the principle of another, as from the species of embryo

---

[160]Cf. pp. 69-70, vers. 103-106.
[161]Cf. p. 70, vers. 107-110.
[162]Cf. p. 71.
[163]*Ibid.*: "Neque est possibile . . ."
[164]*Loc. cit.*: "Si longitudo . . ."
[165]Cf. p. 72.

one can gradually pass on to the species of animal or of man.[166]

Bruno related his doctrine on the variability of things in nature and on the impossibility of precisely determining the sizes of things to the affirmation that the majority of minima forms genera, in which the present genus is contained in the preceding one. Every genus is the realization of that of which the antecedent order gives us a glimpse. This is as true of the various genera as it is of individuals of the same genus. Consequently, "in the human species appear the species of all living beings, more clearly and with more evidence than in other species." E.g., the species horse bears a certain resemblance to the species man as well as to the species ox, dog, jackass, ape, and sheep; among plants this resemblance is more hidden, but it is there nevertheless. It exists here more, elsewhere less, here simply, elsewhere in a complicated manner, as this ought to occur according to various numbers and degrees of complexities. Only an absolute madman can believe that nature employs the relations of numbers that we employ; that it divides numbers into even and odd, equal and unequal, that it goes from decad to decad, from hundred to hundred, and that in all things nature proceeds in a similar manner.[167] To the wise, it is certain that the relations of numbers and methods of calculation are as diverse as the fingers, heads and intentions of those who calculate. Therefore, that which is in agreement with the numbers of nature can never correspond to the numbers we use. Therefore, differences of equality and inequality that seem to us small, insignificant, external or non existent can hardly have anything in common with imperceptible differences.[168] Hence, ten men and ten horses, evaluated by the same number, are not actually equal.[169] Nothing variable and composite can at two moments consist of equal parts or of parts that are of the same order. The flux of the atoms being continuous in all variable and composite objects, one cannot designate them twice with the same name so that one thing signifies on two occasions one and the same object.[170] Bruno terminates this

---

[166]Cf. p. 71.
[167]Cf. p. 72.
[168]*Ibid.*: "Sapientibus enim . . ."
[169]*Loc. cit.*: "Sic decem homines . . ."
[170]*Loc. cit.*: "Nihil variabile atque . . ."

exposition, which is under direct influence of the philosophy of Heraclitus and Cratylus, by doubting the possibility of determining size: because one cannot determine the maximum, the minimum and the middle point of a quantity, one cannot determine the size of that quantity either. "For how can you expect that, one of these parts being undetermined, the whole or any part could be determined."[171]

Having in this manner reduced mathematical certainty to an illusion of the senses, Bruno makes one more digression, to observe the nature of the soul. (*"Excursio physica ad animae naturam contemplandum,"* chapter 6); here, in inspired and sublime verses, he states that despite universal variability, there is permanence of substance. The soul is the monad, and, as such, it is invariable. "The divine nature of the soul is encountered; it cannot be destroyed by any change, or any perturbation."[172] "For whatever becomes, whatever transforms itself, whatever falls and flees, changes continually; therefore, you must not believe that that is substance."[173] Man must learn to know his nature which is by no means that which brings about movement, time and destiny. The sage will not attribute any great importance to these trifling things, but will regard the world of phenomena as an appearance, and will do his best to live in accordance with his nature; thus his life will become similar to the life of the gods.[174]

After stating definitively that the indivisible substance or the monad is being, and that all the rest is accident or the composite,[175] Bruno gives explanations of "indivisible nature," and establishes strange divisions of that nature. According to him, the indivisible nature is twofold: negative and privative. The indivisible nature which is negative is itself twofold, namely, accidental and substantial. The first, such as voice, sound, sensations of sight, extends itself spherically in its entirety wherever it is; for all the eyes see an entire form, all the ears hear an entire voice; another voice is heard, in contrast, by some

---

[171]*Loc. cit.*: "Si in quanto non est definibile . . ."
[172]Cf. p. 73, vers. 3-4.
[173]Cf. p. 70, vers. 14-15.
[174]Cf. p. 73, vers. 16-22.
[175]*Ibid.*: "Individua sola substantia . . ."

intensively, by others feebly, by some completely, by others incompletely. Substantial nature is the soul which is whole not only in each body but also in the whole horizon of the life of the earth where we also live, and in which we exist. (To this subject Bruno links his very fantastic ideas about the magic cult and magic contact, which hold no interest for us and are medieval par excellence.) Above this soul is the soul of the earth in a larger horizon; finally, the supreme soul of souls is God, the unique spirit that fills all, that, above and outside all order, regulates all and is one, simple, and infinite.[176] The indivisible nature which is privative is the element or substance of plurality; it is of the same genus as plurality. This privative indivisible nature can be distinguished from the negative indivisible nature which is not divisible either according to genus or according to species, either in itself, or by accident. The privative nature itself cannot be divided, but division is carried out within it as within the first and homogeneous part of the continuum. The privative nature is twofold; it is subdivided into (a) the first part of that which is discrete (the number one is the atom for the mathematician, syllable is the atom for the grammarian, discourse for the dialectician, meter for the verse-maker) and (b) the first part of that which is continuous, and which is multiple according to several kinds of continua. Besides, Bruno divides qualities into (a) active qualities (the smallest pain, the smallest sweetness, the smallest color, the smallest light); (b) passive qualities (the smallest triangle, the smallest circle, the smallest straight line, the smallest curved line); (c) neutral qualities (in relation to division: the present; in relation to place: the smallest space; in relation to length and to width: the point; in relation to body: the smallest elementary body).[177] One can say only of the accidents that they change (sensations of sight and hearing do not exist through internal composition and do not disappear through dissolution or through division; these sensations appear and disappear); of all the other indivisible species it cannot be said that they appear or that they disappear; by their intrinsic nature they are eternal, immortal, indissoluble;

[176]Cf. p. 74.
[177]Cf. pp. 74-75.

they are souls, gods, God himself.[178] These divisions are characteristic of Bruno's mode of presentation. Bruno had the intention to deduce from these divisions a classification of science.

Bruno occupies himself next with Plato's affirmation that the
circle is a polygon; more exactly, that the circle is composed of
the straight line and curve (*"Plato circulum dixit polygoniam
totum angulum compositum ex recto et curvo"*). Antiphon[179]
presented this by his squaring of the circle. Because neither
planes nor bodies are continuous, and because the circle is composed of points, it is certain that the circle is a polygon, all the
more as the minima of which it is composed are not in touch
through all their limits.[100] A point is not in touch either with
another whole point or with a part of that point, but, since
they are in touch through the terminus, it is necessary to say
that between two points, between two lines, and between a
point and a line there is empty space; therefore, neither the
plane nor the body is continuous (this was affirmed by Leucippus,
Democritus and by many others). In the circle, where a point
is in touch with another point in such a fashion that they constitute a curved line, the limit of these points is an angle. This
is why it can be said of a circle, which is everywhere equal and
uniform, and in which one can see the inclination towards the
point of departure, that it is an angle. Since one imagines the
shortest line between two points, one can admit that a circle
touches a plane through a definite line, between definite limits,
and that the circle touches a similar circle at two points. Then
one can accept that Plato's circle is composed of the straight line
and the curve. Because the circle is equally distant from the
center in all directions; in the circle, ascent coincides with
descent, and this is why one determines the length of the circle
when one has determined its width, for in the circle these two
dimensions cannot be distinguished, just as in the sphere the
three finite dimensions cannot be distinguished from the center,

---

[178]Cf. p. 75.

[179]Antiphon was a contemporary of Socrates (Diog. Laert., II, 46). He
inscribed an equilateral polygon in a circle, while constantly doubling the number
of sides of the polygon; through this procedure he wanted to arrive at a polygon
the sides of which would be so small, that it would coincide with the circle.

[180]Cf. p. 75, vers. 1-3.

and as in the infinite circle and in the infinite sphere the center
is everywhere, so that there can be no question about dimensions. According to Antiphon, the chord can be divided further,
which is to say, that the sides of the polygon can be multiplied
infinitely many times until the minimum is reached, where the
chord and the arc coincide; therefore, the circle can be transformed into a polygon which is equal to the circle. Antiphon
demonstrates that a curve is so similar to a straight line that,
by starting from either of them, one can trace the other; likewise,
one can trace the line that links the middle point of the one with
that of the other. Bruno undoubtedly thinks that by neglecting
the infinitessimal difference between several minima, the squaring
of the circle can be realized, not absolutely, but approximately
(through the final coincidence of the chord and the arc, the
circle becomes equal to the polygon with an infinite number of
sides.)[181]

Bruno develops in detail his previous thesis that the polygon
and the circle do not increase through the addition of one
minimum alone, and refutes the possibility of equating one figure
with another (chapter 8, pp. 77-83). The circle being composed
of a definite number of parts, it increases in a determined order.
The circle can become larger not when one adds to it a minimum
(the smallest circle) from one side alone, but when one adds
to it six minima (six smallest circles); for the circle does not
grow larger, if its radius does not grow larger at the same time.
The polygon, also, does not grow larger through the addition
of only one minimum, but each side must be augmented as many
times as any one side is augmented (because, if one extends only
one side of a square, the square becomes a trapezium). Each
figure, being composed of a constant number of parts, increases
also in a constant order. Since every figure grows larger through
its appropriate gnomon, different figures cannot be equal.[182]
Bruno repeats here once again that in practice one does not
differentiate between the minima, which can only be distinguished rationally,[183] and he rejects the hypothesis of infinite

[181]See pp. 76-77.
[182]Cf. p. 77, vers. 1-11. See also p. 81: "Adde ut neque quadratum
quadrato . . ."
[183]Cf. p. 79, vers. 56-58.

parts: "It is necessary that you possess certain parts within a certain limit,"[184] he says. The minimum being determined by nature, it is not possible to equate a circle with a square, or a square with a pentagon, or a triangle with a square, or whatever sort of figure it may be with some other sort of figure, because a different number of sides demands a different order and a different number of parts. Just as the species of one number cannot be equal to the species of another number, either formally or really, so we can never equate one equilateral figure with another equilateral figure through their elementary parts. Even when the parts of one figure are numerically equal to the parts of another figure, these parts cannot be equal to one another in the size and number of elementary parts.[185]

Consequently, the triangle, composed of three minima, can never become equal either to the square, composed of four minima, or to any other figure.[186] We know already that polygons increase through the addition of odd numbers of parts, and that the circle increases through the addition of even numbers of parts (although it is composed of an odd number of parts). This being the case, *the circle and the polygon can never become equal in the strict sense of the word, just as an even number can never become equal to an odd number.*[187]

By means of the number of parts through which one performs the addition, one can easily arrive at the number of added parts

---

[184]Cf. p. 80, vers. 86-89.

[185]Cf. p. 81.

[186]*Ibid.*: "Sicut enim ex primis partibus . . ."

[187]See *Art. adv. Math.*, pp. 55-56. "Since the circle is not infinite, the polygons which it contains cannot be infinite, whether they be imagined as inscribed or as circumscribed. It is necessary to suppose that circles, as well as polygons, are finite, but one must not believe that the sides of the polygon are equal to the parts of the circle. For, the incommensurability of the polygon with the circle results from the evenness and oddness of parts. No equilateral polygon can be composed of the same number of parts as the circle. The largest polygon inscribed in a circle has to be equilateral, but the circle is greater than that polygon by a third of the parts (according to the number of parts in the circumference and in the sides) . . . As one kind of number is not equal to another kind of number, one equilateral polygon is not equal to another equilateral polygon." "The more angles a polygon, inscribed or circumscribed, has, the more it resembles a circle, but it can never equal the circle." (pp. 59-60). "Squaring a circle is as impossible as equating an odd number with an even number."

which compose a similar figure. It is obvious that one must add the gnomon of nine equal and similar parts to the square the last gnomon of which is composed of seven parts; every other figure is to be augmented in the same order.[188]

One can carry out a non-artificial and ageometrical transformation by constructing a cube, or a pyramid, a sphere or some other equilateral figure of the same wax or the same lead whenever that material is rarified, condensed, compressed or extended in various ways, but this procedure is incorrect, because one does not take into consideration that in every new figure one obtains a different size of voids and pores which cannot be perceived by the senses. "It is a sign of a thoughtless and coarse spirit to accept the arguments for equality or any other evaluation put forward by those who proceed in a similar manner."[189]

Bruno underscores the incorrectness of the transformation of every triangle into a rectangular triangle, of the latter into a parallelogram, and, finally, of the parallelogram into a square. He acknowledges that in the fourth book of this work (*De Principiis Mensurae et Figurae*) he reduced every figure to the triangle; next, that he reduced triangles, circles and other figures to a triangle, to a circle, and to a figure, and that he acted "according to the manner and custom of the vulgar;" but he adds that, from the mathematical point of view, this procedure was used in order to present the things in a more easily understandable manner. However, that procedure has no real value, because one cannot evaluate the elementary parts which are not perceptible.[190] Actually, Bruno profoundly believes that in exact geometry the number of parts of one sort of figure cannot have anything in common with the number of parts of another sort of figure. "The principles utilized in practice differ from the principles of theory; the former are in conformity with nature, the latter are in conformity with the quality of our mind."[191]

In the ninth chapter (pp. 84-85) Bruno explicates the proposition already formulated, that body does not touch another body

---

[188]Cf. p. 82.
[189]*Ibid.*: "Inartificiosam ageometricamque transfigurationem, . . ."
[190]Cf. pp. 82-83.
[191]Cf. p. 83.

or plane either in its entirety or through one of its parts (*"corpus neque se ipso neque parte sui tangere corpus vel planum"*).

The scolia of this chapter contain a new and rather confused affirmation about the terminus. The end (terminus) also has its parts, like the body itself; the smallest body has the smallest part of the terminus through which the other minimum is touched. The smallest body cannot be touched either by a larger terminus or by a smaller terminus, because by means of the termini, through which contact is effected, that which is touched becomes equal to that which touches.[192] Therefore, an atom necessarily touches another atom through the smallest terminus.

Bruno returns to the determination of the nature of the terminus which he examines this time in detail (chapter 10, pp. 85-86, in relation to p. 44). When speaking in a precise manner, one must not say that a line touches a point. Likewise, it is false to say that the extremity of one line touches the extremity of another line, or, for that matter, that the extremity touches a plane; it is more precise to say that the line touches another line through its extremity, because the atom alone does not touch another atom, but, as previously presented, it touches another atom through the terminus, which is between the point of one atom and that of the other. Consequently, the contact occurs by mediation, through something else. One extremity does not touch another extremity, one terminus does not touch another terminus, because, by its nature, a terminus is not that which touches, but rather, it is that through which contact takes place. Thus it is, that the line, the smallest part of width, is connected through its terminus to the terminus of another line, since one cannot conceive any part of width between the terminus and the line.[193]

In the following passage Bruno tries to specify the relationship of the terminus to empty space. There is contact of a point with another point, and not contact between the termini; rather, the contact occurs by means of the terminus; more precisely, by means of the double terminus, evidently as that which serves

---

[192]Cf. p. 85.
[193]Cf. p. 86.

as limit to two adjacent points; hence as that which serves as the meeting place of the termini. Since the termini of two surfaces which touch each other do not make a continuum, one can see that between two surfaces there is indivisible space, called by Democritus empty space interjected between bodies; for between atoms, however tightly compressed, there has to be empty space because the extremity of one atom is different from the extremity of the other, and, except for the indivisible atom which is without parts, one can imagine nothing truly continuous.[194]

If someone were to say that the termini, through which parts are in touch, are themselves in touch, and were asked where or through what they are in touch, he could not answer easily. For, if he admitted that this is in touch through something else, which actually participates in the touching, he would obtain an infinite number of that which touches and of that through which contact takes place.[195] Hence, on the supposition that the termini touch each other, one obtains a *progressus in infinitum.*

Then, Bruno shows the order in which the center diminishes through the augmentation of the circle and of the sphere. As indicated in the plane of Democritus, a circle is in touch with six equal circles, between which there are six angles or, more exactly, six triangles around the same center. This is why the learned antiquity reduced all contact to twelve intervals. It is evident, from the physical, as well as from the geometrical point of view, that the center diminishes in a regular manner: after having placed around a minimum six minima, one places twelve more; so, the whole complexity consists of nineteen parts, namely, of eighteen circles around the central circle.[196] Afterwards, around these parts, one puts other parts in the same order. However, in the infinite, repeats Bruno, returning to his favorite thesis, the center is nowhere, in other words, it is everywhere.[197]

---

[194]*Ibid.*: "Est igitur tactus puncti cum puncto, . . ."

[195]*Loc. cit.*: "Ea vero quibus aliqua se attingunt, . . ."

[196]Cf. p. 87.

[197]Cf. p. 83. In *Art. adv. Math.*, the fourth axiom about the sphere is the following: "The infinite sphere has a truer center, because its center is everywhere; a finite sphere has a truer circumference because in the division of a plane, the circumference is everywhere for him who divides the continuum to infinity" (pp. 14-15). The fifth axiom states: "A finite sphere has no center; for him who divides to infinity, the infinite sphere has no circumference" (p. 15).

At the end of the chapter, Bruno declares once again that the smallest circle touches an equal circle at a point, and that the smallest sphere touches an equal sphere also at a point. The contact is the larger the larger are the circles and the spheres.[198]

The twelfth chapter (pp. 88-89) contains the proposition that of two circles, one being larger, the other smaller, and which are moving in the same plane and at the same speed, the larger circle traverses the plane more rapidly than the smaller circle, because it leaves a larger trace.[199]

Bruno gives here, in connection with that which he treated in the preceding chapter, a definitive statement as to the manner in which circles are in touch: in the plane the contact of each circle with another circle is not equal, but proportional to the size of the circles. The smallest circle touches another circle of the same size through the same part of its extremity as the largest circles touches another equal circle. This becomes clear when one takes into consideration that the greatest curvature is in the minimum or atom, and that there is no curvature in infinity.[200]

We proceed to the thirteenth chapter of the second book (pp. 89-91), which is the most important in this work. It is usually considered that two straight lines, intersecting at a sharp angle ("when a straight line obliquely intersects another straight line"), touch each other at a point. Actually, these two lines touch each other not at a point but at a length.[201] Bruno demonstrates again the falseness of the supposition that straight lines can be drawn between all the points of a figure. One admits that in a square, where the minima or other parts are arranged regularly and at regular intervals, the parts in the diagonal touch each other as much as the parts in the sides. Actually, in square ABCD the atoms (the minima) are in touch in a continuous manner from A toward B and D and not from A toward C. For the little squares turned from A toward B and D touch one another mutually through the sides and are continuous; and the squares turned from A toward C, and from B toward D, are in

---

[198]Cf. p. 88.
[199]*Ibid.*: "Quamvis ergo aequali velocitate . . ."
[200]Cf. pp. 88-89.
[201]Cf. p. 91.

touch through the angles. One finds the opposite in triangle
EFG.[202]

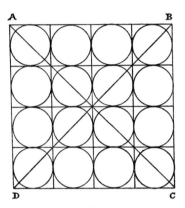

The Field of Democritus

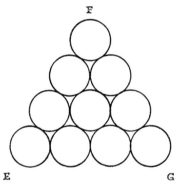

The Equilateral Triangle of Democritus

In the square, then, the continuity of the homogeneous parts,
which is to say of the minima (circles), does not follow the
diagonal but the sides. One can see, therefore, what should be
said in reply to those (Bruno thinks primarily of Aristotle) who
want to conclude from the fact that the points of line AB disappear directly into line CD, by cutting the diagonal AC, and
that there is nothing between a point and another point directly

---

[202]Cf. p. 89.

following the first one, that the points of line AB are equal to the points of line CD as well as to those of line AC, respectively, that the square's diagonal AC is, therefore, equal to its side AB. In their opinion, there is no reason for the diagonal of the square to be longer than the side of the square.[203] Bruno thinks that such an objection against the construction of lines and figures from points can be raised only if the difference between the minimum and the terminus is overlooked. As soon as that difference is grasped, it becomes obvious that the points in the sides of the square touch each other and that those in the diagonal do not. Consequently, the points in the diagonal are more distant from each other than the points in the sides.

Hence, the diagonal of the square is in no way equal to the side of the square, as affirmed by the adversaries of the composition of lines from indivisible points, but is greater than the side. Likewise, only six radii go from the center of the circle toward its circumference, because the smallest circle is touched by six equal circles, as shown in the plane of Democritus.[204]

Bruno criticizes the assertion (based upon the fact that the circle touches the plane at a point) that a straight line is equal to a curve when the circle turns upon a plane, if one supposes that the circle and the plane are composed of an infinite number of parts (chapter 14, pp. 91-94). Through continuous movement all the points of the circle are in direct touch with all the points of the plane; hence, there can be no movement away or swerving that could lead the miserable adherents of the infinite to the conclusion that the infinite parts of the curve exceed the infinite parts of the straight line, because every point on one line corresponds to a point on the other.[205] As soon as one supposes that the plane and the circle are infinite, the conclusion is called for that the movement covers infinity itself, and this conclusion is as correct from the physical point of view as it is from the mathematical.[206] But, according to Bruno, these suppositions are false: "for this reason it is better to trust the senses, in order not to

---

[206]Cf. p. 92, vers. 9-16.
[203]Cf. pp. 90-91.
[204]Cf. p. 91.
[205]Cf. p. 93.

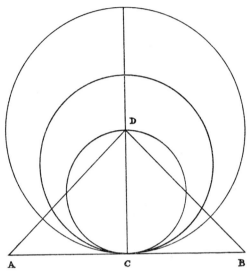

A   C   B

drown in the treacherous river of errors,"[207] and conclude that
the circle and the plane are composed of finite parts and that
the termini, by means of which the parts are in touch, are also
finite. The minimum of nature being very far from the minimum
that can be perceived by the senses, the minima and the termini
are indeterminate, but not infinite.[208] Beyond all is the infinite,
the true, the being unique and good, the monad, the essence
and the existence of all things.[209]

The proposition of Euclid that the smallest circle, the circles
smaller, medium, large, larger, etc. touch line AB (or the plane)
always at a point, is refuted by Bruno in the last chapter of the
second book (pp. 94-96). According to that proposition, the
more the circle increases, the more the points of intersection,
where lines DA and DB cut it, are removed from point D, and
the closer they are to points A and B; but, however large the
circle, it is not possible for it to touch apexes A and B of the
angles at the base, because, in that case, the circle and the line
would coincide.

"I am much astounded by their grievous stupidity as I am
astounded by the stupidity of him who, on the principles of the
same kind, admits that two lines, extended to infinity, can never
meet, though they approach each other more and more . . .,"

[207]*Ibid.*, vers. 28-29.
[208]See p. 94: "Melius ergo . . ."
[209]Cf. p. 93, vers. 48-50.

says Bruno.[210] He resolves this difficulty by affirming that the large circle does not touch the straight line at a point, but that their contact is linear.[211]

Bruno's intention to deduce the true doctrine from a small number of evident truths is voiced in the first chapter of the third book (*On the Invention of the Minimum*). The state of philosophy in his epoch does not satisfy him. "By engaging in intellectual games, which are but affectations, the sophists, long ago, violated the simplicity of philosophy which is invulnerable, and they did this by the multiplication of books and studies, by way of various superstitions, through some digressions and some questions and through the novelty of useless demonstrations. They are succeeded in our time by a deluge of grammarians swollen with presumption and conceit . . . who are regarded as chiefs and leaders of jackasses . . . and who introduce into philosophy an extreme confusion, as the invulnerable Ceneus was crushed by the centaurs under an enormous heap of rocks and wood."[212] In this chapter Bruno again glorifies the Sun which lights the whole universe, pours the elements of life, and reflects the large in the smallest. He prays to the Sun to inspire him with true elements of measure, in order that wisdom, suppressed for such a long time, might be re-established anew.[213]

The second chapter (pp. 98-104) contains a minute explication of the proposition that all plurality increases through the minimum and can be decomposed into minima. (*"Ex minimo crescit et in minimum omnis magnitudo extenuatur."*) Not to take the minimum into consideration means to neglect the measure truer than all others; then, the measure "withdraws completely annihilated and, under a false name, abandons its measurers, because they no longer differentiate between lying and measuring."[214] In spite of everything, the substance of quantity and the elements of measure will remain eternal.

---

[210]Cf. p. 96.

[211]In *Art. adv. Math.*, the first axiom about the circle is the following: "The smallest circle touches a line or a plane at one point, a small circle at a small number of points, a larger circle at several points, and the largest circle at all points" (p. 14).

[212]Cf. p. 98.

[213]Cf. p. 97, vers. 1-14.

[214]Cf. p. 99, vers. 3-7.

In his fantastic manner Bruno states that there are two kinds of geometry which differ as truth differs from a lie, science from ignorance, light from darkness; one of these kinds of geometry is based upon the minimum adapted to man's instruments; and the other, on the unknown minimum; the one pushes myriads into horrible detours, confusions and irregularities; the other is resplendent in a light which enlightens all. "On the part of the former one," says Bruno, "in the introduction to an edition of the Elements of Euclid, one of the censors shouts at the top of his lungs, in this manner, to the naive reader: 'As soon as Democritus and Leucippus suppose the atoms and the indivisible corpuscles, and Xenocrates, certain indivisible quantities, the foundations of geometry are certainly ruined and turned completely upside down, and, once these foundations are demolished, I certainly do not see that there remains anything other than the sudden collapse of the vast theatre of mathematicians. And will so great a number of theorems of geometers on the asymetrical and irrational quantities thereby be destroyed, God willing? How will you explain the reason that an indivisible line measures that line and cannot measure another? Because the minimum found in one genus is the measure common to all genera.'" Bruno replies to him thus: "Must I consider, oh most illustrious sir and master, that it is better to lament because of the ruin of irrationality and incommensurability, than to rejoice in the rebirth of rationality and measure?"[215] By observing the field of Leucippus and the plane of Democritus, one can arrive at the knowledge of the measure which starts from the minimum.[216] Bruno repeats what he said earlier about the enlargement of figures by gnomons and develops his assertion that, from the center of a circle, one cannot draw, toward its circumference, an infinite number of radii, but only six radii, and no more. The number of parts composing the radius will be the number of groups of six parts which enter into the composition of the circumference itself: there is first of all, the radius composed of one minimum, when six circles are placed around the central circle; then, the one composed of two minima, the circle

[215]Cf. p. 102: "Sic igitur duo geometriae genera, . . ."
[216]Cf. p. 103.

consisting of twelve parts; then, the one composed of three minima, corresponding to the circle of eighteen parts; finally, when the circle has twenty-four parts, the radius is composed of four minima, etc. Thus, the fact that parts of the circumference are multiplied by number six can serve as a point of departure for new divisions of the arc.[217]

When one supposes that the sphere is regularly composed of small spheres, one can determine its surface, the size of its largest circle being known. If the largest circle of the sphere is composed of twenty-four minima, the surface will consist of sixty-one minima; if the largest circle is composed of eighteen parts, the surface will be composed of thirty-seven parts; if it consists of twelve parts, the surface will have nineteen parts; finally, when the largest circle of the sphere has six parts, the surface is composed of seven parts. When the circumference is composed of a single minimum, the surface of the sphere is also composed of a single minimum, or, as Bruno puts it: "A part which contains only itself, and nothing other, remains homogeneous."[218]

Not only the circle, but every other figure also grows in a determined order, starting from the minimum, and diminishes in a determined order to the original minimum. According to this, the surface of every figure can be evaluated. *Bruno admits that the surface of a figure is equal to the sum of the minima of which it is composed.* Therefore, in the evaluation of the surface of a figure, Bruno does not take into consideration the termini, because he supposes them without any size.

Bruno regarded as rational only the division of the circle into real parts (according to the rule by which one first puts around a minimum six minima, then twelve, etc.).[219] In brief,

---

[217]*Ibid.*: "Ut quot partium . . ."

[218]Cf. pp. 103-104.

[219]Because one places around one minimum six other minima, it follows, in strict adherence to things, that the figure increases in the form of a hexagon; hence, the infinite alone can have a perfectly circular form, because sphericity coincides in an absolutely perfect manner only with infinity. See *Art. adv. Math.*, "The minima being thus placed around a minimum in order to fill space, they double the circumference and increase continuously in the form of a hexagon; for this reason only the infinite can be physically circular, and that, in a simple manner" (p. 23). "The plenum in a circle composed of elementary parts is a

by supposing the minimum determined, one arrives at the surest method of division and measure; on the contrary, on the supposition of proportional parts which can be taken as being of whatever size, one does not arrive at any definitive result.[220]

Every angle can be divided into only two parts (chapter 3, pp. 104-106). "It is astonishing how the new geometers, the most stupid among those who bear that name, admit that the angle must be divided into innumerable parts . . .,"[221] says Bruno. The minima being circular, one can draw from the center of a circle only three diameters or six radii,[222] and, from the summit of an angle, one can trace only one line. Every other division of angles is false and incorrect.[223]

Consequently, the center is not the limit of all lines departing from the circumference (chapter 4, p. 106-108). It is believed, without reason, that the number of lines departing from the center toward the circumference is the same as the number of minima from which the circumference is composed, and that one thus avoids empty space. He who desires to know the order in which the circle expands, in other words, the number of lines that can be plotted from the center, should recall that which is indicated by the plane of Democritus. What was previously said about the difference between the minimum and the terminus is more than sufficient, as Bruno thinks, for every spirit not ab-

---

[220]Cf. p. 103: "Et quid prodest per partes . . ."

[221]Cf. p. 105.

[222]"They make a mistake, when they terminate all the lines departing from the circumference with the indivisible center. We have indicated that a point or an atom can be touched only by six points or six atoms . . . For around the middle atom one admits a circumference composed of six minima of a twofold kind, just as the genus of minimum is twofold" (p. 23). "As already said, geometers think very stupidly that the center of the circle terminates all diameters" (p. 60).

---

hexagon; the void in a circle composed of elementary parts, most closely approximating the circle, is a hexagon of another kind. Therefore, the smallest circle touches the center which is the smallest part; it is composed of three hexagons of two kinds" (pp. 60-61). It would, therefore, be impossible to divide a circle, in the strict sense of the word, because the center is the indivisible minimum.

[223]"Trying to divide the center, which is the limit or, more exactly, the middle minimum, by calling it an angle, amounts to a useless endeavor, which is worse than idleness. Where a minimum is touched by lines, it is necessary to observe the minimum which fills space with six other minima placed around it" (*Art. adv. Math.*, p. 32).

solutely devoid of insight.[224] Once this difference is understood, all controversy about the number of lines departing from the center toward the circumference becomes useless; then, one realizes that only six lines attain the circumference.

The fifth chapter (pp. 108-109) presents Bruno's idea that a minimum must be supposed in every kind of work, however great the minimum may be. From among many parts, one takes as the minimum the one which is indivisible by the instruments and for the eye.[225] Upon examination of the previously presented and the following, it will become clear how one can conceive the sensorily perceptible minimum as that which descends towards the imperceptible through the mediation of the perceptible; or as that which ascends through the perceptible to that which is the largest. Then, it will also be clear how equal parts grow and in what orders of intervals the determined parts are in touch.[226] "It is not worth while to write the prolific lists produced by an extreme ignorance of our century, when all the light of the art of measuring is extinguished," cries out Bruno. "Soon, without exceeding the limits of the triangle, I shall chase this darkness away; I shall explain the essence of being and the origin of light, in order to reveal the foundations of the true wisdom with which God had illuminated the world, and to shed light upon the most worthy things, for, as we have already said, in the minimum is that which is greatest."[227]

Ignorance of the minimum is the mother of the teaching about irrational and asymmetrical quantities. (*Doctrinae de alogis et asymmetris matrem esse ignorantiam minimi*, chapter 6, pp. 110-111.) All controversy about irrational and asymmetrical quantities results from the ignorance of the minimum as well as from the fact that all division of quantity is subjective and subject to the will of the one who divides. From the practical and mechanical viewpoint, quantities are divided now into even parts, now into odd parts, because the elementary parts are not perceptible and because one confounds them in a certain kind of

---

[224]Cf. p. 108.
[225]*Ibid.*, vers. 1-3.
[226]Cf. p. 109.
[227]*Ibid.*, vers. 16-24.

resemblance. Thus, in coarser tasks, one cannot distinguish the minima; for example, when one has to divide a measure of grain into parts, one does not perform the division according to the number of *minima*. In more subtle activities, the geometers notice this difference, but do not accept it, due to a lack of principles, and so continue to measure with the measures that are closest to them.[228]

Bruno, then, categorically denies that one can measure in a manner of certainty without the knowledge of the minimum. He who counts numbers, takes, at will, a number for the measure of other numbers, instead of taking for the point of departure of his evaluation, the elements of numbers, the monads. "Thus, this one is the measurer as much as that one is the counter; both are as close to the art of number and measure as darkness is to light and truth to a lie."[229]

In the seventh and eighth chapters (pp. 111-119), Bruno rejects the tables of curves and then establishes four methods of determining the part of a totality: the first method is by means of straight lines, the second and the third are by means of the rectangular triangle, and the fourth is by means of the equilateral triangle.

Although the minimum is not perceptible, Bruno does not lose hope of reaching the truth about it. When one recognizes that the whole is composed of a definite number of parts, one thereby recognizes each of the parts, as Bruno naively tells us. If the whole consists of two groups of six parts, the part occurs in the whole 2 X 6 times; if the whole consists of 2 X 8 parts, the part occurs in the whole 4 X 4 times. The half is contained in the whole two times; the third, three times, etc.[230]

The figure represents the first method of investigation for determining the size of the part of a whole. First, the division of the line into elementary parts is shown; then, such a part is divided into smaller parts; finally, the new parts are divided into still smaller parts, etc. The further one moves from the first parts toward the second, from the second towards the third, etc., the

[228]Cf. p. 111.
[229]Cf. p. 110, vers. 25-27.
[230]Cf. p. 112, vers. 17-26.

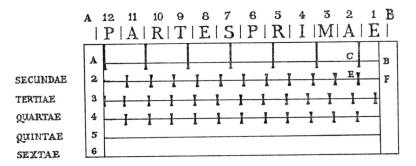

smaller the parts become. Any part of the first part stands in relation to the entire first part as the first part stands in relation to the whole; likewise, any part of the second part stands in relation to the entire second part as the entire second part stands in relation to the first part; and as the first part stands in relation to the whole. The same is true of the third, fourth, fifth, sixth, and, finally, of all the other parts of parts. It is clear, then, that in a line composed of twelve parts, a part is contained twelve times, that half of that part is contained twenty-four times, its third, thirty-six times, etc. If one asks for any part of the first part, one will take part AC which is contained twelve times by the line, the first parts of which are PA, AR, RT, etc., or indeed, if necessary, one will take that part doubled or tripled.

If one asks for the third part of a line divided into twelve parts, the third part will occupy the four parts which will then be called four secondary parts. If the requested part is larger or smaller than the primary part, one then reports the remainder of that part or of the larger part, in order to terminate the division.

Bruno remarks that this operation is performed above the same line on which the primary parts are designated. He used accessory lines to explain this operation better.[231]

The second and third methods consist in the transposition of parts on one side of the rectangular triangle and in tracing similar triangles. (Bruno presents these two procedures as well as the fourth one, in an extremely confused manner, in chapter 8, pp. 115-119.)

[231]See pp. 113-114.

The fourth method is the best: "it is the zither of the Graces, which represents the elements of measure and from which proceeds the sea of things and all harmony . . ." This method is "the sun among the measures" (*Sol inter mensuras*), since the sun reveals itself and other things. According to the fourth method, the parts are discovered by means of the equilateral triangle, in which parallels to the sides can be drawn with the greatest ease.[232]

Having established that the circle is composed of a finite number of minima, Bruno shows the uselessness and incorrectness of the rules of spherical triangles (chapter 9, pp. 119-121).[233] Trying to represent a model of the sphere in the plane is senseless; it is as mistaken as seeking the reason of the plane in the sphere. The figure should be considered in the form appropriate to it, but one must not conform to practical usage, or take the rational norm,[234] because the middle point of the chord is not the middle point of the arc.

The geometers seek a refuge in the division of the circle into infinite parts, but the matter does not in that way become any clearer. Actually, on this supposition of infinite parts, the confusion becomes still greater.[235]

Bruno's obscure language in the scolia of this chapter is aimed at expressing that the norms valid for the division of the arc in the sphere are not valid for the division of the arc in the plane.

In spite of this, Bruno undertakes the division of the arc of the circle (chapter 10, pp. 122-124). By means of the radii, he first divides the circle into six triangles, and, afterwards, the side of the triangle into as many parts as are necessary to divide the arc.

In the following chapter (pp. 124-127) he presents three procedures for determining which part of the circumference represents the given arc. These are jugglings with geometrical notions, rather than serious propositions, so that it is absolutely

---

[232]See p. 119.

[233]"Where measurers revert to this paltry art of triangles, and to pictures of curvatures and chords, the loss of measure is clear and obvious; they look, with a lantern, for a lost brain" (*Art. adv. Math.*, p. 29).

[234]Cf. p. 120, vers. 19-26.

[235]Cf. pp. 120-121, vers. 40-46.

useless to embark upon their explication. Bruno has already lost much of the seriousness of exposition which he kept developing with difficulty up to this point.

Further on (chapter 12, pp. 127-128), Bruno intends to discover the common measure (*Communem mensuram inveniam*). He is of the opinion that the sure way to discover the common measure is provided by the minimum. In that passage there is also a critique of the doctrine of irrational quantities. "The doctrine about the irrationals will not help you, and you will remain a measurer without a measure. Rules must not be uselessly multiplied, because no invention will result from them and for a measurer, the measure which is appropriate to him, suffices."[236]

The heterogeneous measure common to two straight lines is the circle (for example, when one looks for the number of times a smaller circle is contained in one with a greater radius). The homogeneous measure is the spherical triangle for the arcs, and the rectilinear triangle (the zither of the Graces) for straight lines. The common measure is twofold: the whole of various parts, which is the indirect measure, and the part of various wholes, which is the direct measure. An example of the primary measure is the number twelve. Twelve is the common measure of all the numbers contained in it: it contains eleven and the eleventh part of that number; it contains ten and its fifth part, etc. An example of the secondary measure is the number three. Three is the common measure of all that is composed of six, nine, and twelve parts. The elementary common measure is one, namely, the minimum which is twofold, the simple minimum occurring in nature; and the minimum in genus, which, in turn, is also twofold: the minimum that can be perceived by the senses and the minimum that can be perceived by reason.[237]

---

[236]Cf. p. 127, vers. 13-16.

[237]Cf. p. 128.

See *Art. adv. Math.*, pp. 66-67. "Admitting that in every genus the minimum is the measure, it is certain that vulgar geometers have no measure, because they have no minimum. When we establish the minimum, the foundations and the edifice of geometry are set up. The most famous theorems about asymmetrical and irrational quantities are destroyed, because there is no reason for which the indivisible line would measure one line and would not measure another. Quite obviously, from this truth result innumerable advantages as much for him who

The deductions we have just cited do not really represent any mathematical discovery; they are mentioned only to round out the exposition.

Bruno tries to show in a fanciful way the order in which the circle is divided; he gives parts of the circle names such as foyers, chambers, spaces, etc. (chapter 13, pp. 128-129).[238] He thought by this procedure to have replaced the tables of curves, and invented a method for measuring every circle and every arc.

The fourth book contains the exposition of the principles of measure and figure (*De principiis mensurae et figurae*). The first chapter (pp. 130-135) deals with the development of the monad, which creates, first, the small number, then the large number and afterwards proceeds to that which is innumerable and infinite (*Progressio a monade ad pauca, inde ad plurima usque ad innumera et immensum*). This chapter is distinguished by the seriousness of its subject and constitutes one of the most remarkable parts of the work. Pythagoras[239] had raised the monad to the tetrad and lowered the tetrad to the monad; he taught that the monad becomes the dyad, that the dyad becomes

---

[238]See *Art. adv. Math.*, p. 70. "How will one divide a circle in a regular and continuous manner for the purposes of astronomical, geographical and mathematical works? I do not say that one should make use of the indeterminate and indefinite trouble of mathematicians and of archivists, but of the geometrical and continuous subordination of parts. I admit that a circle can be divided into 12 regions or residences, each residence being divided into 12 foyers, each foyer into 12 orders, each order into 12 chambers, each chamber being divided into 12 sides, 12 spaces, 12 offices, 12 residents, 12 species, 12 members, 12 articles. Thus, we admit the existence of similar and analogous parts of the same order, as much in name as in reality, and follow the order of nature which divides; another manner would not correspond either to the first or to the second order of nature, but would always be opposed to it."

[239]Bruno believes that it is his duty to avenge Pythagoras for the false accusations by Aristotle. He cannot forgive the latter for having refuted "*platonicas ideas et pythagoricos numeros.*"

---

investigates from the mathematical perspective as for him who explores from the physical point of view. The common measure is twofold, to wit, a common part which, for a known reason, is contained within the two totalities, and a common totality which, for a known reason, contains the two parts. An example of the first measure is the number three which is common to nine and twelve, because it is contained in the first number four times and in the second, three times. An example of the second measure is twelve, which is common to the numbers three, six, four and two; because it contains three four times, six two times, four three times, and two six times."

the triad, and that the triad becomes the tetrad. Hence, the monad is the limit and number of things.[240] Bruno accepts this conception of Pythagoras: the monad, the dyad, the triad and the tetrad are the principles of all things. It goes without saying that the monad is the first principle: the dyad is composed of two monads; the triad, the first odd number, is composed of three monads; finally, by adding the monad to the triad, one obtains the tetrad. The sum of the monad, the dyad, the triad and the tetrad yields the decad which limits all numbers and is the number of numbers.[241] Delighted to have given a rational explanation of the origin of numbers, Bruno says: "But it is first necessary to bow before the sanctuary of the sacred spring and pour the first libations, now that we have succeeded in reducing the infinite species, in which we had wandered, to certain definite species of nature understood by a similar spirit. One can see from this that all numbers are in the monad both actually and potentially."[242] Consequently, number, which derives its origin from the monad, increases in a certain order. Thus, nature provided the first foundations for art, which forms similar species. Other numbers, including even the infinite number, are composed of these elements.[243]

Bruno makes the same deduction from the geometrical point of view. "Having then terminated our examination of the minimum as the monad in genus, we should not, here, disturb the order, but should, on the contrary, say a few things about the development of the point, by which one designates the first dimension of quantity."[244] There exists first the minimum in the form of a point which is the image of the monad (the number one). When the point moves towards the second limit or second

---

[240]Cf. p. 130, vers. 1-5.

[241]Cf. p. 131, vers. 17-23.

[242]Cf. p. 132, vers. 28-34.

[243]*Ibid.*, vers. 34-38. In his work *De Monade, Numero et Figura* Bruno, following the example of the Pythagoreans, gives a numerical image of the world. The monad is the principle from which all proceeds; the dyad is the principle of opposites from which plurality results; the triad makes the opposites return to the original harmony; the tetrad is the symbol of perfection, because the sum of the first four numbers gives the decad $(1+2+3+4=10)$; the pentad represents the number of external senses, etc.

[244]*Loc. cit.*, vers. 24-27.

terminus, it forms a line which is the image of the dyad (the number two). The line limited by a terminus or by two termini does not enclose anything, limit anything or form anything. When the line reaches the third terminus, the line forms a triangle which is the principal figure of one kind; when one terminus of the line turns around the other terminus until it has resumed its first position, the terminus forms a circle, the principal figure of the other kind. Thus one obtains from the point, which is the image of the monad, the first triad (the straight line, the triangle and the circle), which is the principle of all figures.[245] Hence, the movement of the point forms the straight line, the movement of the straight line forms the plane, and the movement of the plane around a center forms the sphere. In other words, the movement of the point produces the dimension of length, the movement of the dimension of length yields that of width, and the movement of the dimension of width produces that of depth. One has not arrived at the genus of the fourth dimension, because at a point of the sphere (the center) only three diameters can intersect: the first one represents length, the second, width, and the third, depth.[246] "The threefold diameter intersects at one point, so that the right angle remains always constant."[247]

In departing from the teaching of Xenophanes that the universe is one, unique and absolute, and from that of Parmenides who descended from divinity toward nature and ascended through nature back toward divinity, Bruno establishes that particular things derive their origin from the monad, which is existence, the most common and the most general; being; the absolute truth; the source of the world of plurality and diversity.

Since all things have the same origin, one cannot say that a thing which exists differs from another thing to such an extent that each does not remain similar to the other in a few points.

---

[245]Cf. p. 134.

[246]*Ibid.*: "Primum fluente puncto est linea recta, . . ."

[247]Cf. p. 131, vers. 15-16. See also *Art. adv. Math.*, p. 36. "Although a line has only the dimension of length, it represents, nevertheless, all the differences of dimensions; in the circle, as well as in the square, the line represents length and width. In the sphere, where the three dimensions are indicated in the same manner, and where they are the same, the line also represents depth."

We do not see anything opposed to any other thing in the elements of nature, except that which coincides with another thing in the same desire, and especially in the desire for self-preservation.[248]

In this passage Bruno takes note of the struggle for self-preservation in nature in an absolutely optimistic manner (*"bellum omnium contra omnes"*). He mentions this fact in passing, but does not see the possibility of great dissonance in the midst of universal harmony.

Therefore, nothing in the universe is so tiny that it does not contribute to the integrity and perfection of the whole. There is nothing that, evil for someone and somewhere, is not at the same time good and excellent to someone else, somewhere else. Hence, nothing shameful, evil or inconvenient happens to him who looks at the universe; variety and oppositions do not disturb the universal good; nature directs all, just as the choir-master directs all the contrasting voices, the low and the high, and reconciles them in the best symphony that one can imagine.[249] The resemblance between the various phases of the monad is manifest also in geometry, in line, triangle and circle.[250] Bruno

---

[248]Cf. p. 134.

[249]Cf. p. 133.

[250]"The infinite straight line is a circle, because it is a circumference with an infinite diameter. In it the beginning cannot be distinguished from the end, because its center is everywhere. In the infinite triangle, the sides and the angles are equal; there, the three lines become a single line, and the three angles become only one angle; consequently, the infinite triangle becomes a circle." "The side of the infinite triangle is equal to its angle. This triangle has, of necessity, equal sides and angles. Besides, it has one angle and one side. Furthermore, in it the angle and the side are identical. Moreover, it is a line. In addition, it is an angle or, rather, it is a circle. Why is this trinity a unit? Because, in this trinity, three lines and one line, three angles and one angle are identical" (*Art. adv. Math.*, pp. 44-45). In short, in the infinite circle the diameter and the circumference coincide perfectly; thus, the infinite circle becomes a straight line. "In the infinite circle the diameter and the circumference are identical and become of necessity one and the same line; the infinite circle is in that way the infinite straight line" (*Art. adv. Math.*, p. 59). In infinity, where possibility and reality coincide, a line cannot be distinguished from a body, because it has the possibility to become the body. Being potentially all, infinity is motionless; because nothing can be distinguished in it, everything in it is one. Because in infinity point cannot be distinguished from body, or center from circumference, or that which is the largest from that which is the smallest, Bruno asserts that the infinite universe has no center; more exactly, that

calls this resemblance "coincidence of dimensions" (*coincidentia dimensionum*).

From all that has been said, it follows that the knowledge of the minimum is indispensable to the knowledge of mathematics, physics and metaphysics, because the metaphysical minimum comes out of its absolute existence, either as the monad that is found somewhere, or as the physical atom or as the point.[251]

It is interesting to note that, like Pythagoras, Bruno believes that by studying mathematics one can penetrate the secrets of nature.

Bruno demonstrates that the three elementary figures, namely, the straight line, the triangle and the circle, contain other figures not only implicitly but explicitly as well (chapter 2, pp. 135-137). He calls the first, Apollo, the second, Minerva, and the third, Venus. The circle and the triangle are the measure of each other; at the same time, they represent two figures that are the largest and the smallest. The largest triangle is circumscribed around and the smallest one is inscribed in the circle. The circle carries the inscribed triangle but is itself inscribed in a triangle. The circle is the measure of measures and the figure of figures.[252]

In the third (pp. 137-139), fourth (pp. 139-141) and fifth (pp. 142-143) chapters, Bruno devotes a foyer to each of his elementary figures; these are the foyers of Apollo, Minerva and Venus (he intended thus to mark the importance of these figures). But the interpretations of each foyer are allegorical, puerile and without any geometrical value. Bruno did his best to create decorative figures; he was not bent on their being geometrically justified. It should be remarked that these three deities represent three fundamental ideas: the good, the true and the beautiful.

Next, Bruno presents his geometrical definitions (chapter 7,

---

[251]Cf. p. 134.
[252]Cf. p. 135, vers. 10-15.

---

its center is everywhere, and that its circumference is nowhere. "For us, the universal sphere is a continuous, infinite and unmoving universe in which infinite spheres or particular worlds are situated" (*Art. adv. Math.*, p. 72). To the Inquisition these ideas seemed to represent "horrenda prorsus absurdissima" (altogether the most absurd of horrors).

pp. 144-148). The first two are the *general* definitions of the minimum and the terminus.

The minimum is that which has no parts but is the first part. *The terminus* is the limit which has no parts, but is itself not a part.

The following two definitions are those of the minimum and of the terminus as points.

The first part of the plane which has no parts is *the point which is the minimum*. *The point terminus* is the point that limits every part but has no parts.[253]

Among other definitions the following ones are characteristic of Bruno's geometry:

The smallest line is the uninterrupted continuation of a point in length; it is the elementary part of a plane.

The line terminus is the line which has no parts and which represents the uninterrupted continuation of a point. It is the limit of body and surface.

The surface is the limit of the body, a limit that has parts in length and width.

The atom is the minimum of the body; it has length, width and depth and can be a part as well as a terminus.

The atoms lined in a simple longitudinal manner compose *the line of the body*. This line may just as well be part as terminus of the body.

The part is that which is smaller than the whole; *the whole* being that which results from the composition of all the parts.

The measure evaluates the size of the quantity: the minimum is its limit.

That which remains is *larger* and *unequal;* that which is neither larger nor *smaller* is *equal.*

The straight line is the shortest distance between two points; *the plane* is that which is limited on all sides by straight lines.

The gnomon is that which, added or subtracted, enlarges or diminishes a figure without changing its form.

The circle is the plane the circumference of which is always equidistant from the center along the radii.

---

[253]Cf. p. 145, vers. 9-14.

The sphere is the body which has equal length, width and depth and the limit of which is circle.[254]

The twelve axioms of Bruno are pronounced by twelve mythological personages (Orestes, Pylas, Amyntas, Hermes, etc. chapter 8, pp. 148-150). We shall cite the following ones:

The one is the reason of the one, the similar of the similar, the equal of the equal, the opposite of the opposite, the inverse of the inverse.

A thing is similar and equal to another thing, when it coincides with that other thing qualitatively and quantitatively.

If one subtracts a quantity equal to two quantities or adds a quantity equal to each of these two, the remainders or the sums would be equal if the quantities were equal, and unequal if the quantities were unequal.

The whole is greater than the part, and the part is smaller than the whole.

If two quantities are equal to a third qualitatively and quantitatively, they are equal to each other qualitatively and quantitatively.[255]

The theorems of Bruno are also pronounced by various personages (chapter 9, pp. 150-152). We shall cite only the one according to which every plane figure is composed of triangles, and can be decomposed into triangles, just as each body is composed of pyramids and can be decomposed into pyramids;[256] for his other theorems are confused combinations of the definitions and propositions of Euclid.

Afterwards, Bruno gives a bizarre demonstration of his theorems, inventing absurd analogies between mythological personages and geometrical figures (chapter 10, pp. 153-158).

The fifth book deals with measure (*De mensura liber*). This book is the most confused and most foreign to scientific exposition; if one leaves out all the fanciful digressions it contains, only a few serious things remain.

Bruno speaks of the straight line, the angle and the triangle. He finds the archtype of the truth (*veritatis archetypus*) in the

---

[254]See pp. 145-147.
[255]See pp. 148-149.
[256]Cf. p. 152, vers. 27-28.

straight line. A line drawn between two points is the shorter, the straighter it is; hence, the straight line is the shortest distance between two points. Between two points one can draw an infinite number of curves, but they are all longer than the straight line. So, truth is one, simple and the most easily comprehensible; a lie is multiple, complicated, difficult, similar to the geometry and philosophy of the sophists.[257] "For this reason Anaximenes said that that which is dispersed in numbers and in matter is void and non-being, and Melissus and Parmenides said that the single being is alone true."[258]

At this juncture, Bruno establishes that a threefold measure exists: the measure above the thing and before the thing (the one, the spirit, the idea); the one in the thing and with the thing (size, weight, movement); and the one behind the thing and outside the thing (the efficient, the formal, the instrumental).[259] He also gives a few subdivisions, even more devoid of importance than the divisions. Then, he repeats his idea about the continuous flux of things in nature, and about the impossibility of finding in nature two equal things and evaluating them (chapter 2, pp. 161-162). Further on (chapter 4, pp. 163-164), one comes across the assertion that the limit (the terminus) of length is perceptible, although the minimum of length is not. We can perceive the line which is the minimum, because it is marked in the plane by the difference between two colors.[260]

Not wishing to dwell upon the futile and irresponsible passages immediately ahead, we shall cite only a few that seem to us of some value.

After one has determined the minimum, the first part, not every line can be divided into two equal parts, even if one conceives this minimum indistinctly and confusedly. On the contrary, when one sets up divisibility to infinity, then there

---

[257]Cf. p. 160: "Linea brevissima . . ."

[258]*Ibid.*, vers. 25-27.

[259]*Loc. cit.*: "Mensura triplex . . ."

[260]"Lineam quae est terminus indicat duorum in plano colorum differentia, eam vero quae est minimum nullo possumus sensu comprehendere" (p. 164). See *Art. adv. Math.;* p. 36. "How can length be perceived without width? By perceiving that line in a plane which is the terminus and the difference between two colors."

are neither first parts nor middle, nor ultimate parts, but only indeterminate ones which can be divided at will.[261]

According to Bruno, the angle has a fourfold significance: the angle is, to begin with, the terminus as a point; next, the minimum linking the extremities of two lines; then, the distance between two lines (between the extremities of two lines?), designated by the names of obtuse, right and acute angles; finally, according to a special signification which Bruno gives it, and which plays a considerable role in the invention of the minimum, the angle is the measure of the triangle.[262]

The smallest angle is situated between the convexities of two circles in mutual touch;[263] the larger the circles, the larger is the angle, but the sides of the angle become with it also correspondingly more rectangular. When the circles become the largest, the angle is the meeting place of two straight lines. Therefore, the smallest and the largest are determined by the magnitude of the curvature because the greatest curvature occurs in the smallest circle, a smaller curvature in a larger circle, and the smallest, in the largest circle. But Bruno points out that this opinion is actually false, because there is no reason for the straight line and the curve to coincide.[264]

From the nature, order and disposition of the minima, and making use of the triangle of Leucippus, Bruno demonstrates that the angle can be divided into only two parts.

He proceeds to the glorification of the triangle that was raised to heaven by Mercury. "It seems to me that the triangle has every right to be included among the celestial figures because every figure emerges from the triangle and because each can be

---

[261]Cf. p. 166. See also *Art. adv. Math.*, p. 35. "Since the same line can be divided into equal parts and into unequal parts, and since the parts are taken to be of some magnitude or other, I admit that one does not divide the line, but that it is taken already divided."

[262]Cf. p. 177. Compare with *Art. adv. Math.*, p. 41. "I conceive of the angle in a triple sense: it is a terminus which is not a part, but which, also, has no parts; or the minimum which is the first part, or, yet, the distance of one of the parts (on the base or on the arc of the circumference), taken from the point of encounter of two intersecting lines."

[263]Compare *Art. adv. Math.*, p. 44. "How can one draw the smallest angle? By taking the angle situated between the convexity of two circles in touch with each other."

[264]See chapter 7, pp. 180-181.

decomposed into the triangle and the triangle itself cannot be decomposed into any figure as its first part."[265] In order to emphasize the importance of the triangle, Bruno naively says that in the oracle of Delphi there used to be a tripod and other objects triangular in form.

The triangle and the circle are the principles of all figures, as the pyramid and the sphere are the principles of bodies. The triangle is the largest of the figures that contain the circle, but at the same time it is also the smallest of the figures that are contained in the circle. Consequently, it become clear that the triangle is as much the minimum as it is the maximum in relation to the circle and to all other figures. In moving from the circle to the polygons, the first figure is the triangle, which is, therefore, closest to the circle. In moving from the triangle to the square, to the pentagon and to polygons with an increasing number of sides, all the way to the circle, one can see that, of all the figures that are contained by the circle, the triangle is the most distant from it. In relation to the triangle and other figures the circle is, therefore, the largest as well as the smallest. Between the circle and the triangle there is an interconnection such as there is between matter and form, potentiality and actuality, that which can be limited and the limit, the container and the contained, the minimum and the maximum.[266]

As the smallest angle emerges from the contact of two circles which are the smallest, so the smallest triangle emerges from the contact of three circles which are the smallest. The smallest figures proceed from the contact of the minima, because the smallest void exists between the smallest bodies.[267]

Tangled constructions of triangles in the circle are not worth the difficulty of presentation. Bruno accumulates nomenclatures, bizarre figures and superficial analogies till the last chapter, devoted to the art of Lull[268] (*De occulta scriptura*, pp. 208-218),

---

[265]Cf. p. 188, vers. 9-12.

[266]Cf. p. 190.

[267]Cf. p. 191, vers- 10-17. See also *Art. adv. Math.*, p. 28. "How does one obtain the smallest triangle? From three smallest circles touching one another."

[268]Raymond Lull (1235-1315), Spanish scholastic of the XIIIth century, famous alchemist and inventor of a kind of topics and mnemonics, consisting of pictures of ideas which were supposed to facilitate meditation on all subjects. Several works of Bruno are devoted to the exposition of this art which he links to his metaphysics (the clearest among these works is *De Imbris Udearum*).

for whom he had a particular predilection. Instead of shedding light upon his ideas, as was his intention, he tangles them to incomprehensibility. A spirit exclusively intuitive, Bruno loses his way wherever a logical or mathematical deduction is necessary. The remark made by Tiraboschi applies here: "I do not believe that this system can be understood even by the most subtle genius, or that it can be read to the end even by the most patient man."[269] Brucker thought, without a doubt, of the end of *De Triplici Minimo,* when he said that this work was "more obscure than a dark night" (*atra nocte obscurior*).

---

[269]*Storia della lett. ital.,* vol. XI, p. 435.

Chapter III

CRITIQUE OF BRUNO'S DOCTRINE OF THE MINIMUM

AT FIRST GLANCE, it seems bizarre and inexplicable that Bruno, starting from his doctrine of the infinite and limitless universe, should have been able to arrive at the conception of elementary and indivisible parts of matter, taken as the principle and substance of all that is composed and divisible. After refuting Aristotle's arguments that upward the world is limited,[1] Bruno begins to explicate and argue his thesis that matter in the universe is finite. He does this, perhaps, because he had intuitively sensed the veracity of that idea, and also, perhaps, because of his conviction that whatever had been taught by the founder of the peripatetic school was false, and, accordingly, even his deductions of the infinite divisibility of matter.

From our interpretation of the subject of the work *De Triplici Minimo*, it follows as certain that it is to Bruno that the

---

[1]Bruno's refutation of Aristotle's arguments, and his numerous metaphysical, physical and theological arguments in favor of the infinity of the universe can be found not only in his work *De l'Infinito Universo e Mondi*, but also in *De Immenso et Innumerabilibus*. According to Aristotle, the finiteness of the universe must, of necessity, be deduced from the perfection of the universe, and because infinity cannot be perceived by the senses. In opposition to this, Bruno asserts that, with the senses, we can never perceive a phenomenon as ultimate, because every phenomenon presupposes another phenomenon; moreover, the hypothesis of a finite universe cancels out the goodness and greatness of God. As for Bruno's other arguments, we shall merely call attention to them. The conclusion to which these arguments lead is that each thing, wherever it may be situated, is always in the center of the universe, in other words, that the center of the universe is everywhere.

credit belongs for the first attempt at a detailed construction of a new geometry, which the modern finitist, Petronijevic, later called discrete geometry. This geometry, which, for the sake of greater simplicity, we shall designate as discrete geometry, supposes *space to be a finite discretum composed of simple and indivisible points.* As a metaphysician, Bruno recognized that *discrete geometry* is much simpler than *continuous geometry* and much more closely related to metaphysics. It is for this very reason that he embarked upon the critique of continuous geometry and the construction of discrete geometry. Let us say at once that Bruno was so intensely aware of this relationship of geometry to metaphysics, that he found it impossible to make purely geometrical deductions.

Having distinguished the metaphysical minimum, the physical minimum, and the geometrical minimum, he was unable to consider one of them independently of the others. In the development of his geometrical considerations, he would lose himself in seemingly unnecessary digressions detrimental to his geometrical system. Furthermore, Bruno, on several occasions, discovers for a moment a truth, but, immediately thereafter, covers it again with quantities of phrases bearing no apparent relationship to it and rendering the comprehension of that truth more difficult.

Bruno rightly regards the minimum as the substance of things and the supposition of the threefold minimum (the atom, the point, the monad) as indispensable to a well-ordered foundation of the natural sciences, mathematics and metaphysics. Faithful to the viewpoint of his theory of the first principle of things, the minimum, Bruno develops his critique of the infinite divisibility of space. That critique is subtle and ranks among Bruno's rare logical passages; it demonstrates that, despite numerous puerilities with which his works are filled, Bruno is a philosopher of genius.[2] He judiciously holds that, like the division of numbers which must stop at the number one, not lending itself to any further division, so the division of matter, however large it may be, must stop at the indivisible atom. Matter and number are finite downward and infinite upward; number can be added to number, infinitely many times; likewise, the addition of parts of matter can be

---

[2]Cf. Brucker, *Historia Philosophiae*, tome IV, p. 32.

pushed to infinity; in other words, when parts are being added to matter, itself composed of atoms, and to number, composed of units, one can go on to infinity, but, when matter and number are being divided, one necessarily arrives at the indivisible part.[3] But it is not only by division that one can arrive at indivisible parts. These parts exist *prior* to the division and *independently* of it. Ignorance of the minimum—in other words, downward division of space to infinity—causes a great confusion in the natural sciences as well as in mathematics.[4] This is why it is necessary to establish definitively that the number one (the monad) is the essence of every number, that the atom is the substance of every body, and that the point is the substance of every geometrical figure.[5] In this connection, Bruno's sketch, according to which even infinite and eternal time consists of indivisible moments, is characteristic.[6] Unfortunately, Bruno does not particularly dwell upon this idea.

Bruno's critique of the infinite number is not sufficiently convincing or precise. Starting from the fact that, in the domain of infinity, the part is identical with the whole, and that there can be no difference in that domain between that which is larger and that which is smaller, Bruno concludes with reason: if in the infinite number even one number were finite, no number could be infinite.[7] Nevertheless, from Bruno's complete explanations, it follows that he was not in a position to understand that one cannot, in any fashion whatever, attain the infinite number by the multiplication of the finite number.

In more modern terms, Bruno was unable to discover the contradiction of the infinite number. This is why, in spite of that critique, the concept of infinity remains fundamental in the philosophy of Bruno.

---

[3]Cf. *De Tripl. Min.*, p. 22.

[4]See Bruno's Latin text quoted under footnote 61 in chapter II of this volume.

[5]". . . monas est essentia numeri . . . Ad corpora ergo respicienti omnium substantia minimum corpus est seu atomus, ad lineam vero atque planum minimum quod est punctus" (*Op. cit.*, p. 10).

[6]". . . duratio est aeterna a parte anteriori ante hoc et post hoc et quodlibet temporis quod accipias instans, ad quam sane omni procul dubio hoc instans vel tempus quo scribo finis est" (*Op. cit.*, pp. 22-23).

[7]Cf. pp. 24-25, vers. 26-27. Also: p. 26, vers. 84-86. and p. 31.

The principal part of the work *De Triplici Minimo* consists in the exposition of the manner in which the minima are mutually attached. On this subject, Bruno makes a great and fortunate discovery by which, once and for all, he justifies the possibility of *discrete geometry*. The initial supposition from which one must start in order to avoid Aristotle's objection that space cannot be composed of indivisible points, because placed side-by-side, they would coincide, that is to say, could not realize the extension of space, is the supposition of two kinds of points; the ones which are the smallest parts of discrete space, and the others which are the points separating these parts in such a fashion that they do not coincide. Bruno clearly realized the need for making this supposition, and therein lies his great merit. He was the first to establish the existence of two kinds of points in discrete space: *minima,* the smallest parts of which that space is composed, and *termini,* located between two minima, serving as points of contact to these minima, and separating them so that they do not coincide. A minimum does not touch another minimum either in its entirety (because it would thus coincide with that other minimum) or through any of its parts (because, being the last and indivisible part, it has no parts), but a minimum can touch several other minima through its limit (its terminus). That which is valid for the minimum considered as a point of a line is also valid for the minimum as an atom of a body. The atoms are not in direct touch, the terminus being between the atoms as their limit.[8] *Therefore, by establishing the difference between the minimum and the terminus, Bruno brilliantly succeeded in conquering the greatest difficulty raised against discrete space.*

Bruno devotes a minute analysis to the notion of the terminus. The minimum and the terminus are two kinds of the smallest: the minimum is that which touches, it is a part, while the terminus is that through which contact of parts takes place, therefore, their limit. Bruno excludes the supposition that one terminus can touch another, and that quantities can be augmented by means of termini. Apart from termini linking points,

---

[8] Cf. pp. 29-30.

Bruno distinguishes three more kinds of them: the termini linking lines with one another, those linking surfaces with one another, and, finally, those linking bodies with one another. There are no termini infinite in quantity; where parts are not infinite, either actually or potentially, there cannot be an infinite number of limits to the parts (although, at first glance, one might imagine so, given that by the division of parts, the termini can be multiplied, but not divided). On the other hand, there cannot be any more termini than there are parts, if for no other reason, because a terminus occurs between two points.[9] All these observations are precise and keen.

We are going to try to express clearly that which Bruno did not put into a final form, but which he seems to us to have implied in his geometrical considerations: this is, that the size of the minimum equals one, and that the size of the terminus equals zero.[10] In this idea, let us say it at once, consists the principal error of Bruno's discrete geometry; here lies the cause of his failure in the development of that geometry, which he was obliged to reduce to a few formulated reflections. Because he had supposed the magnitude of the terminus equal to zero, Bruno was obliged to imagine empty interstices between the minima of surfaces and the minima of bodies. In the plane, between circular minima, there are interstices in the form of curvilinear triangles; in the body, between spherical minima,

---

[9]Cf. pp. 30-31.

[10]In *Articuli adversus Mathematicos*, p. 24, Bruno says explicitly that a minimum of empty space (a terminus) is smaller than the minimum of plenum (a minimum in the proper sense). (Minus minimo dari in natura intelliges atque senties, ad diversas minimi species inspiciens. Plano enim minimo quod est ut plenum minus est minimum quod est ut vacuum; de solido quoque minimo, ut pote tridimensionato vacuo, idem est iudicium.") This seems to be in absolute contradiction with the assertion on p. 30 of *De Triplici Minimo*, according to which the terminus is not smaller than the minimum. ("Inquies stupide: ergo datur minus minimo, quandoquidem hoc, quo minimum tangit minimum, est minus. Nequaquam, amice, sed tuo te more confundis. Hic duo sunt minimi genera, et eius quod tangit, id est partis, et eius quo fit tactus, id est termini.") In short, this last assertion is meant, perhaps, only to underscore more strongly that a minimum and a terminus are two different kinds of minima. Bruno draws all his geometrical conclusions as if he understood the magnitude of a terminus to equal zero.

there are interstices in the form of pyramids with curved planes.[11] According to this, the first parts of matter consist in voids and plenums which cannot pentrate one another at all. The terminus, which represents no quantity but is identical with empty space, cannot have a dimension; it is, rather, the principle of dimension, the point of departure of a dimension.[12] Altlhough Bruno himself thought to have discovered the process of rationally exploring the enlargement of figures through the introduction of empty space, in addition to full space, in the construction of discrete geometry, he made a mistake in the sense of thus identifying his theory of mathematical atomism with the theory of physical atomism.[13] Actually, the minima of Bruno, even when he treats them as mathematical minima, as points, always remain atoms of the physical continuum. Bruno could not conceive of non-spatial nature (in the sense of indivisibility), but he attributed to it spatial forms. Mathematical minima are not, for Bruno, *"vanae species mathematicorum;"* this is why he does not differentiate between these and physical bodies. The mathematical minima correspond to physical atoms; the termini, situated between the minima, correspond to physically empty space. According to Bruno, this empty space is filled with limitless and invariable ether present in all bodies (Bruno calls it *"spiritus universi"*).[14]

Briefly, in discrete geometry Bruno is to be praised for having invented the notion of the terminus and in no way for having given its explanation. All of Bruno's attempts to enter more closely into an interpretation of the nature of the terminus and specify its connection with empty space, have remained vague and indeterminate.

According to one passage in Bruno, it would follow that minima are in touch through two termini, and not through one alone. Having established that whatever is composed is formed by a juxtaposition of minima and can be decomposed into minima, while the minima themselves cannot be either composed

[11]Cf. p. 47.

[12]"Terminus est principium dimensi et unde seu de quo . . ." p. 49.

[13]See K. Lasswitz, *Geschichte der Atomistik*, vol. I, pp. 381-391.

[14]Bruno's conception of ether differs from that of the modern natural sciences, because Bruno rejects in nature all mechanical action.

or decomposed, Bruno says: "If this is so, they are in touch through two termini appropriate to them, and not through one alone, because contact occurs between two termini, and this is why Democritus asserts that empty space occurs between bodies."[15] In all probability, Bruno had the same thing in mind when he said: "It is in this manner that a line, the smallest part of width, is attached through its terminus to the terminus of another line, since one cannot conceive any part of width between the terminus and the line."[16] Further on, Bruno says:. "There is, therefore, contact between point and point, and no contact between termini; rather, there is contact by means of the terminus; more precisely, by means of the double terminus, evidently as that which serves as limit to two adjacent points, as well as meeting place for the termini."[17] Since the termini of two mutually touching surfaces do not make a continuum (the atom alone, having no parts, is continuous), Bruno draws the conclusion that between two surfaces there is indivisible space, which Democritus called empty space interjected between bodies; because between the atoms, however tightly compressed, there must be empty space, the end of one atom being different from the end of the other.[18]

The manner in which Bruno understands the touching of the minima by means of two termini remains, therefore, perfectly indefinite. In his most frequent and most limpid formulas, it is a question of the minima being in touch through only one terminus. Evidently, Bruno identifies the interstices situated between his minima with empty space, because in his capacity as a still early thinker, he lacked the option to conceive a more abstract explanation of the terminus. But even this identification itself is not well defined by him. According to all the evidence, Bruno does not feel that his definitions of the terminus are definitive, because he constantly returns to them. There is, after all, nothing surprising about this poet of the infinite worlds not

---

[15]Cf. *De Tripl. Min.*, p. 44.
[16]*Op. cit.*, p. 86.
[17]*Ibid.*, p. 86.
[18]Cf. *Loc. cit.*: "Cum quippe duorum . . ."

having the power to explain the essence of the terminus *more geometrico.*

At all events, it is certain that Bruno fills the interstices between his minima with ether in order to avoid the objection of Aristotle, because, if the interstices were not filled, they would not be capable of separating the minima. *Bruno no longer conceives the ether-filled interstices between the minima as a discretum, but as a continuum.* Therefore, having supposed the size of the terminus equal to zero, he introduces a contradiction into his construction of discrete space.

After showing the fundamental error of the system of Bruno, we are about to continue our critique of the important results at which he arrived in the work just analysed.

Bruno's finding that the form of the minimum of the plane is the circle, and the form of the minimum of the body, the sphere,[19] is the result of his identification of mathematical minima with the physical atoms of the continuum.

Since the minima of Bruno are circular (spherical) in form, since, as we know, between the minima of surfaces there are spaces triangular in form and between the minima of bodies spaces pyramidal in form, he rightly observes that every surface can be decomposed into triangles and every body into pyramids.

With reason, and in conformity with the elementary postulates of discrete geometry, Bruno deduces the impossibility of drawing straight lines between all points of a figure. In this manner, he averts in principle the difficulty raised by Aristotle against the possibility of figures being composed of indivisible points, because every line being composed of points, the length of the line would have to equal the number of points composing it; then the diagonal of the square would be equal to the side of the square. *According to Bruno, the minima composing the diagonal of the square are more distant from one another than the minima composing the side of the square.* More exactly, the diagonal of the square is not a real line, because lines can be drawn within a figure only if there is a continuous succession of homogeneous parts (of minima).[20] By continuous succession Bruno

---

[19]Compare with the Latin texts cited in the preceding chapter.
[20]Cf. p. 90.

understands the shortest distance between two minima separated by a terminus. Just as in a figure with straight lines it is impossible to draw lines from all sides, so in a circle it is impossible to draw an infinite number of diameters (radii), because the smallest circle, the circle consisting of a single minimum, expands when 6 minima are added to it, then 12, 18, etc. Hence, in every circle, however large it may be, it is possible to draw only 6 diameters.[21] For the same reason, an angle can be divided only into two parts.

In the development of the idea as to the impossibility of identifying one geometrical figure with another, Bruno demonstrates great logical capacities; his arguments are simple and clear. It is certain that a triangle, composed of three minima, cannot become identical with a square, composed of four minima. Next, as with polygons increasing, according to Bruno, by odd numbers, and the circle by even numbers, it cannot be doubted that polygons can never become equal to circles, just as odd numbers can never become equal to even numbers. It must not be forgotten, Bruno particularly insists, that both *polygons and circles consist of a finite number of minima;* it is only the difference in the finite numbers of the minima of which they are composed that renders impossible their equality.[22] His demonstration of the incorrectness of transforming one figure into another is equally justified. Nevertheless, he himself employed these transformations, familiar in geometry, because this is permitted in practice.

On the other hand, Bruno's approach which consists in taking into consideration only the minima in the calculation of a surface, is false. Since Bruno's termini are identical with empty space, since they have no size, Bruno considers the surface of a figure equal to the sum of the minima contained in that figure. On this topic the geometrical system of Bruno has been corrected by modern finitism.

---

[21]Cf. p. 91.

[22]In the opinion of K. Lasswitz, Bruno himself infringes upon the established rule according to which the number of minima of one kind of figures cannot have anything in common with the number of minima of another kind of figures; the triangle which comes into being with the seventh gnomon, and the square which comes into being with the fifth gnomon consist of the same number of minima (36 minima) (*Geschichte der Atomistik*, vol. I, p. 374).

The minimum cannot be perceived by the senses, as Bruno rightly noted. But he mistakenly says that neither can the perfect circle be observed by the senses, because at the boundary of the circle with the surrounding space, one can see a perfect circumference. That generalized statement leads to the view that the perfect circle does not exist even in nature, and aims at representing the difference between infinity, where there are no more opposites, and the world of phenomena, where there are opposites and differences (for, with the exception of atoms which remain always the same, everything in the world, says Bruno, undergoes incessant transformation). According to him, it is idle even to seek in nature regular geometrical forms identical with each other, or, for that matter, identical with themselves at two different moments. This application of the *"panta rei"* of Heraclitus to geometry is exaggerated and wrong.

Bruno's distinction between mathematical quantities and quantities appearing in nature contains the seed of the mathematical empiricism of Mill. Bruno destroys the mathematical theory of rationalism with his affirmation that the relations of numbers and methods of calculation are as different as the fingers, heads and purposes of those engaged in counting. It is impossible to find a precise manner of determining quantities, when the minimum cannot be perceived by the senses.

Bruno discovered—it is necessary to emphasize this once again —that the line which is a terminus is indicated in the plane by the difference between two colors. Only, he was unable to exploit this discovery to save the apodicticity of mathematics from the empiricist point of view. Bruno mentions Sextus Empiricus[23] as a representative of empiricism in the domain of mathematics. The latter denied the possibility of perceiving a single dimension in isolation from the others, as Mill was to do later. Contrary to this, Bruno did find it possible to perceive the pure dimension of length in the boundary line, but he could not draw from this the conclusion that independently of the fact that the science of mathematics derives, and must derive, its origin from experience, mathematical propositions remain,

---

[23]*De Tripl. Min.*, p. 164.

nevertheless, apodictic. In any case, Bruno demonstrates a remarkable power of penetration, although he merely sketches the aforesaid truth. Just as Bruno does not clearly conceive the difference between rationalism and empiricism in the theory of knowledge in general, so he could not establish the difference between rationalism and empiricism in the domain of mathematics.

That power of penetration of Bruno's is confirmed also by his distinction among four kinds of angles and by his statement that the smallest angle is to be found between the two smallest circles in mutual touch, and the smallest triangle among the three smallest circles in mutual touch.

Among Bruno's geometrical definitions, in addition to those of the minimum and of the terminus, as points and as lines, the ones characteristic of discrete geometry are the definitions of the atom, the line, the body and the gnomon, though the last three are not original. The axioms and theorems of Bruno are embroiled in mythological digressions and poetic licences, but, once they are deciphered, it becomes apparent that the only one of significance for discrete geometry is the theorem in which Bruno tries to demonstrate the decomposition of every plane figure into triangles and of every body into pyramids, as their elements.

Bruno's attempts to replace tables of curves by some new and simpler process of measuring are absolutely without value. But the idea, which he especially emphasized, that it is not permissible to evaluate spherical forms in a plane or plane forms in a sphere, is perfectly correct from the point of view of discrete geometry.

Bruno's account of the manner in which the monad develops into a dyad, the dyad into a triad, etc. shows how much he was under the influence of the Pythagoreans. Analogous to the formation of the first three numbers, Bruno, as we have seen, presents the formation of three elementary geometrical figures (the straight line, the circle, the triangle). It is true that in these three elementary figures all the others are present, either implicitly, or explicitly, but the manner in which Bruno demonstrates this cannot be taken seriously; this is playing with ideas, making forbidden jumps from geometry to mythology, which may lead one to believe in the accusation that with Bruno the knowledge of mathematics was not at all solid.[24] Yet the cause of these puerilities would not be the ignorance of mathematics, but rather Bruno's inconstancy and lack of system, further augmented by his exercise of the art of Lull. This art has notably developed in Bruno an inclination toward murky figures of speech. It is interesting to observe that Bruno's numerous geometrical considerations end with the introduction of the infinite upwards and with the idea that infinity is also spherical in form, that in the sphere of infinity the center is nowhere, which is to say, that it is at every point, etc. The idea of the infinite universe being predominant in Bruno's intellect, he could not dwell, for any length of time, upon the explanation of the finitude of the ultimate parts of matter and of figures (as we already know, the conceptions of the ultimate parts of matter and of the ultimate parts of figures are not sufficiently distinct in Bruno). The notions of the indifference between all opposites and of the coincidence of dimensions are Bruno's general metaphysical ideas, cited in the present work only in passing. But let us remark that where Bruno is the most eloquent is when he speaks of the disappearance of all opposites in infinity, when he talks of the coincidence of the line and the circle, the triangle, the circle and the line, etc.

Bruno's conception of discrete space may have been clearer than it appears in the form he gave it. The proof of this is his continual repetition that the triangle is the elementary geometrical figure. With this last remark we have exhausted almost all that is essential and important in the work *De Triplici Minimo.*

By his tendency to simplify geometry, more exactly, to give it metaphysical justification, Bruno showed that he was not merely an enthusiast dazzled by the vision of infinite worlds, but that he was also capable of placing the most profound metaphysical problems on their true foundation.

---

[24]According to G. Libri (*History of Mathematical Sciences in Italy,* vol. IV, p. 144), Bruno was not a mathematician; his works contain many geometrical slips.

It is a paradox, we repeat, that the most fervent adherent of the infinity of the universe among the philosophers should be precisely the one who argued the most persuasively that it is necessary to stop the division of matter at the indivisible part, and, equally, that it should be he who conquered the principal difficulty of finitism. Being rather a defender of his ideas than a logician and dialectician, Bruno was incapable of giving a justified system of the new geometry. The role of Bruno in the history of philosophy in general, and of discrete geometry in particular, is great not because he links his ideas systematically, but because he discovers them intuitively.

At the end of this study we shall present in detail the doctrine of discrete space and the construction of discrete geometry of the metaphysician Petronijevic, contemporary representative of finitism, in order to show the final results obtained from the seed which Bruno cast into discrete geometry. We shall start from Petronijevic's theory of space, because his discrete geometry can be directly deduced from it.

Petronijevic rejects Newton's conception of space, according to which empty space exists around real things, as well as Kant's conception, according to which space is the subjective *a priori* form of the sensibility. He accepts Aristotle's doctrine of space, which considers space as the form of the order of being, as the simultaneous givenness of real things.

The first question posed by Petronijevic about the structure of space relates to the finiteness or the infinity of space upward and downward. He confirms what Bruno had also remarked, that the empirical necessity of the ultimate simple parts of space does not exist. Our representation of space upward attains a maximum, impossible to exceed (according to Bruno, our representation of space upward is not closed by any limit); by contrast, in the division of a part of space we arrive at the minimum, which is neither indivisible, nor simple, but is sometimes larger and sometimes smaller. Therefore, according to Petronijevic, as according to Bruno, the simple and real point of space in itself cannot be perceived. It was important to make this statement because there are philosophers (Berkeley and Hume) who proclaimed the *minimum sensibile* as an immediate fact of experience. Petronijevic was, then, forced to confirm the existence of the ultimate parts of space by discovering contradictions in the notion of actual infinity itself. There are three contradictions of infinity: *the contradiction of the infinite number; that of the absolute finiteness of whatever is infinite, and the contradiction of the abrupt passage from the finite into the infinite.*

Before all else, Petronijevic analyses the very idea of number. A number is a sum of simple and absolutely indivisible units. In the order of space, there is nothing that corresponds to the arithmetical unit, the number one; the indivisible *minimum sensibile* not being given in our perception of space. By contrast, in the order of time, the absolutely indivisible instant corresponds to the arithmetical unit. Since in pure time only one unit is always given, the notion of number, as a sum of several similar units, can never emerge from pure time; it is also necessary to make use of the spatial order. In pure space, meanwhile, abstracting all consideration of time, we can bring about the synthesis of number up to three; if we have to deal with a larger number, we establish this by counting in time.

The contradiction of the infinite number consists in the following: every member of the infinite order of numbers is finite, because every member is an outcome of the immediate synthesis of the number one with the preceding number. The infinite number would therefore have to be the last number of the order of finite numbers, which is contradictory. Petronijevic explains this antinomy in the notion of infinite number as issuing from our having arrived at the notion of number by the combination of the order of space with the order of time. In the infinity of the order of numbers one finds the first supposition of the notion of number, the order of time, infinite in itself; in the necessity of the finite order of numbers is to be found the second supposition of the notion of number, the simultaneous order of space. We have seen that Bruno could not even notice this contradiction, let alone resolve it.

Before proceeding to the two other contradictions of infinity, Petronijevic cites direct arguments in favor of the absolute infinity downward, in other words, arguments directed against the possibility of a simple spatial point. In the first place, the simple point, as part of space, is impossible, because its size is zero, and with zeros alone one cannot compose extension; secondly, it is impossible, because two points would have to be in direct touch, and they cannot be, because between them there must be a point which separates them (without this, they would not be two distinct points); and, thirdly, it is impossible, because two points must be in touch, and the contact of two points results in their decomposition into simpler points. Petronijevic destroys these three counter-proofs. The first is not valid because the size of a spatial point, like that of the temporal point, is equal to one, and not to zero. The assertion of the second proof, that between two given points there must always occur a point which separates them, is correct, but the affirmation that this middle point is of the same species as the points separated by it, is incorrect. Petronijevic makes a distinction between the real spatial point, filled with matter, and the unreal spatial point, which, devoid of matter, separates two real points. As soon as this distinction between two kinds of points is made, the difficulty of viewing space as composed of simple points disappears at once. The third argument could have meaning only if every contact were necessarily the same as that between composite units.

If the three cited arguments were correct, absolute continuity of space would result therefrom, and if space were absolutely infinite upward and downward, in other words, if the infinitely small of the lowest order did not exist downward as well as the infinitely large of the highest order upward, the contradiction of the finitude of whatever is infinite would become apparent. If the order of the infinite upward and downward were absolutely infinite, then the finite which is given to us is evidently infinitely small in relation to the infinitely large of the first order and infinitely large in relation to the infinitely small of the same order. It follows from this, however, that every spatial size would in itself have to be finite; its quality of infinity would consist in its being composed of an infinite number of finite magnitudes, which is contradictory. The third contradiction of infinity, the contradiction of an abrupt passage from the finite into the infinite, consists in this: that in the infinite order of numbers it is necessary that through the addition of a unit to a finite number, the number become infinite; yet in this manner, one can only obtain a finite number. This contradiction is illustrated by Petronijevic with the straight line. Line *AB* represents the straight line the extreme points of which, A and B, are infinitely far from one another; in other words, the number of finite parts between A and B is infinite. If we start from point A, given in the finite, toward point B, which is in the infinite, then the number of parts, designated 1, 2, 3, 4 . . . will be infinite, just as the order of finite numbers in the sequence of natural numbers is infinite.

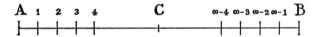

At point B, which is in the infinite, will terminate the infinite number of parts between A and B; in other words, point B represents the last infinite number of finite parts. If one begins to count parts of the line starting from point B, and in the opposite direction, then the first number after B will be $\infty-1$, the second $\infty-2$, the third $\infty-3$, etc.; these are infinite numbers proceeding decreasingly, whereas the numbers in the preceding series proceed increasingly. These two series of numbers going in two opposite directions toward their encounter with one another on the same straight line *AB* will inevitably meet somewhere, for example, at point C. Point C will then be infinitely far from point B, whereas its distance from point A will be finite: point C marks the termination of the series of finite numbers, and, by obtaining the smallest infinite number in adding the number one to the last and largest finite number, the infinite series begins. It is, however, contradictory that by the simple addition of the number one, it should be possible to obtain from a finite number an infinite number. This would be an abrupt passage from the finite into the infinite, and it cannot be conceived, if one accepts the existence of infinite wholes with finite parts. To avoid this contradiction, one must suppose that there exists not only one infinite number, but that there are infinite series of infinite numbers, which actually means the disappearance of the simple unit (the number one). From this, one deduces that, if the order of numbers is to be freed from all contradictions, then space cannot be composed of indivisible parts; hence it must be absolutely infinite downward, or else, if one supposes the order of numbers composed of simple units, space can only be finite, that is to say, a discrete quantity.

Petronijevic illustrates with a straight line the difference between the absolute continuum and the infinite discretum. A continuous straight line is divisible an infinite and absolutely indeterminate number of times. By the division of the discrete line one arrives, by contrast, at simple parts, lending themselves to no further division.

While the three contradictions of infinity are valid for the infinite spatial discretum, the contradiction of the infinite number is not valid for the spatial continuum, because where the ultimate parts are not given, there is nothing to count. In the spatial continuum there exist, however, extended segments of a straight line, and wherever a finite segment passes into an infinite segment, the passage must be abrupt; consequently, the contradiction of the abrupt passage from the finite into the infinite is valid for the continuum. As for the contradiction of the finitude of whatever is infinite, that contradiction is absolutely valid only for the spatial continuum, because, in reality, it makes sense only if space is infinite upward as well as downward.

Of the geomerical arguments against the continuum, Petronijevic takes into consideration the following: the geometry of infinity demonstrates the continuity of space upward and downward. But that demonstration leads to the coincidence of the circle and the straight line, which serves as the basis for the theory of the continuity of space and which is contradictory and impossible. Since it is certain that in the infinite continuum the circle and the straight line *must* coincide and since it is equally certain that they *cannot*, Petronijevic deduces therefrom the impossibility of a spatial continuum. He draws the same conclusion as a consequence of the following argument: the parallels having to meet in a point at infinity, the plane at infinity becomes a point. Then he shows that continuous space cannot have more than two dimensions; as soon as one-dimensional space (the straight line) is absolutely infinite, it transforms itself into two-dimensional space (because the straight line at infinity becomes a circle, and the circle, in its capacity as a closed curve, must necessarily enclose the surface of the circle); this two-dimensional space, being infinite, transforms itself at once into a simple and inextensive point, and that definitively stops all extension into a larger number of dimensions. Consequently, only an inextensive continuum is possible. That being the case, *space can only be a discretum; it can only be composed of simple and indivisible ultimate parts.*[25]

Petronijevic agrees with Bruno's distinction between two kinds of points in discrete space: Bruno's minima correspond to Petronijevic's *real central points;* whereas Bruno's termini correspond to the latter's *unreal middle points.*[26] By hypothesizing two kinds of points, the ones that are parts of space and the others that separate these parts from one another, Petronijevic demonstrates definitively his thesis about discrete space. This thesis appeared impossible as long as one considered only a single kind of points, because the discretum thus kept being transformed into an absolute continuum.[27]

From the metaphysical point of view, one can see an essential difference between real points and unreal points; the real central points are the ultimate elements of real matter, and the unreal

[25] See Branislav Petronievics, *Principien der Metaphysik*, Erster Band, Erste Abtheilung: Allgemeine Ontologie und die formalen Katagorien, Mit einem Anhang: Elemente der neuen Geometrie, Heidelberg, 1904, Carl Winter's Universitätsbuchhandlung. pp. 168-249.

[26] *Ibid.*, p. 250-251. See also *Über die Grösse der unmittelbaren Berührung Zweier Punkte*, Beitrag zur Begründung der diskreten Geometrie, *Oswald's Annalen der Naturphilosophie*, Bd IV, 1905, S. 240. "Den realen Punkt nenne ich Mittelpunkt und den irrealen Punkt Zwischenpunkt, Ausdrücke, die ihren Unterschied, wie mir scheint, klar angeben."

[27] *Principien der Metaphysik*, S. 253.

middle points represent the void in discrete matter: Petroni-jevic distinguishes the *geometrical observation* from *the real observation* of space, though, according to him, the geometrical space coincides perfectly with the real space.[28] He says that predominance should be given to real points as long as real space is being observed in relation to its real matter: if one observes the geometrical structure of space, predominance should be attributed to unreal points, taking these points for units.[29] Not having distinguished two ways of observing space, Bruno considered space only as real. For that reason, the real points, the minima, have a predominant importance in his geometrical constructions.

Like Bruno, Petronijevic affirms that the size of a real point equals the unit (the number one). He presents copious argu-ments in support of the following assertion: The size of the real point must be equal to the unit (one), it must be a real correlate of the simple arithmetical unit, because, equated with zero, its size would signify the absence of real matter, which is impossible. Just as the size of the point must be equal to zero in continuous space, where the division into parts does not really occur, where all extensive quantity is divisible to infinity, and where, accord-ingly, the simple and indivisible point does not exist; so likewise, in discrete space, the size of the real central point must equal one, because there that point exists as the ultimate part of space.[30]

Petronijevic resolves the question as to the nature of unreal points, treated by Bruno in several places. An unreal point is impossible without real points, it is possible only as a point which separates two real points, it is possible only between real points. But, inversely, the real points themselves are not possible without the unreal points which separate them; the supposition of real points inevitably results in the supposition of unreal ones; two real points are not possible without the unreal point between them. This affirmation, which can be directly deduced from the very observation of two points of discrete space in touch with each other, is for Petronijevic a fact of direct intuition.

---

[28]*Ibid.*, p. 252 ". . . der sogennante geometrische Raum mit dem realen Raum als solchem zusammenfällt . . ."

[29]*Ibid.*, p. 252.

[30]See *Über die Grösse*, etc., p. 240.

The question as to the existence of unreal points in discrete space is linked by Petronijevic to the question as to the existence or non-existence of voids in that space. Simple real points of space cannot be separated from one another by unreal and extended voids, because nothingness has no extension at all. The simple real points must, therefore, be in direct mutual touch. Since the unreal voids separating them cannot be extended, *real space must necessarily be a discretum without voids.*[31] The question of knowing whether the size of the unreal middle point is equal to zero or to one seems to Petronijevic of such importance that he makes dependent upon it the possibility or impossibility of the construction of discrete space, and, consequently, the very construction of discrete geometry. His whole argumentation shows that discrete geometry can be deduced without contradiction only by supposing the size of the direct contact of two points, more precisely, the size of the unreal point, to be equal to one.[32]

The first argument cited by Petronijevic in support of the size of the unreal point being equal to one can be deduced from the very notion of an unreal point. The size of the unreal middle point must be equal to one, because, in itself, this point is as simple and indivisible as the real point. Between these two kinds of points there can be no quantitative difference, but only qualitative differences, because the one contains real matter, while the other does not possess such matter. But Petronijevic is aware that, as a result of its equalization with one, the unreal point must be considered a simple void and that this entails a metaphysical difficulty.[33] From its being impossible for absolute nothingness to be extended, he deduced the necessity for a

[31]See *Principien der Metaphysik*, pp. 254-255.

[32]"Was ich nun behaupte und wovon die Möglichkeit der diskreten Geometrie als wirklicher mathematicher Disziplin abhängt, besteht darin, dass die Grösse des irreellen Zwischenpunktes im diskreten Raume ebenso gleich 1 zu setzen ist, wie die Grösse des reellen Mittelpunktes 1 beträgt" (*Über die Grösse*, etc. p. 240).

[33]"Wenn die Grösse der unmittelbaren Berührung gleich 1 ist, dann muss der irreelle Zwischenpunkt eine leere, einfache, nichtseiende Lücke darstellen, und eine solche ist doch unmöglich; die metaphysische Schwierigkeit des irreellen Zwischenpunktes lässt sich also gar nicht verkennen, sobald man nur darüber reflektieren will" (*Über die Grösse*, etc., p. 262).

discretum without voids, but, on the other hand, he recognized that this nothingness cannot be extended in such a way as to represent the indivisible one. Yet, without the unreal point, discrete space is not possible. The empty point, absolutely unextended, which necessarily separates the two real points in discrete space, remains impossible as long as one does not suppose something real that would pose and render possible this void in itself. In other words, the unreal middle point represents a negative kind of reality, because, to be able to exist, it must be filled with a special reality. Petronijevic provides the solution of the difficulty by establishing *that to the unreal point corresponds a real act of negation.* But the real act of negation is not situated between the real points in the spatial sense; it is a point outside space. Hence, in the hypothesis of the act of quantitative negation outside space is to be found the metaphysical reason for the extension of matter.[34]

The second argument in favor of the size of a real point being equal to one is derived from the notion of the unreal middle point, inasmuch as it represents the distance between two real points. From the viewpoint of continuous geometry, the distance between two points is always an extensive line, so that two points in direct touch do not even exist. At first glance, it seems that the distance between two real points in discrete space can only equal zero, if these points are in direct mutual touch. For just as the distance between the extremities of two lines in touch in continuous space is zero, so likewise, it seems that the distance between two real points in touch in discrete space must also equal zero. But the notion of distance in continuous geometry cannot be extended to the space of discrete geometry. The distance between the extremities of two lines in touch in continuous space must equal zero, because, actually, in that space two lines are only parts of a single line, fictitiously divided into two parts by the mathematical point. In the continuum itself, there is really no division, no separation of two lines, that is to say, no separation of their extremities turned toward each other; hence, there is no real distance

---

[34]See *Über die Grösse,* etc., p. 241-242, 260-261. *Principien der Metaphysik,* pp. 255-256, 269-271.

between those two extremities; this is why that distance must equal zero. But it is not the same in discrete space. The extensive and indivisible line of the continuous space is decomposed here into a series of real points in touch with one another. To the continuous and extensive line of the continuous space, a line really indivisible and fictitiously divided by the mathematical point, correspond in discrete space two real points, *really* separated by the unreal point. *To suppose that the inextensive void between two points of discrete space which touch each other equals zero, means to lose sight of the essential difference between continuous space and discrete space.* Two real points in direct mutual touch in discrete space are effectively separated from each other, in the strict sense of the word. The possibility of discrete space can be denied; but once the possibility of the simple real point is accepted, one must also accept that if the points are situated outside each other, if they do not coincide, discrete space can effectively be constructed from these points. If two spatial points are real points only because they are outside each other, separated from each other by the middle point, then the size of that middle point can no longer equal zero, but must equal one. This is so, because in this case the distance being equal to zero would mean that two real points are not even separated from each other, that they are not one outside the other. More precisely, the distance being equal to zero signifies the disappearance of all distance, and, here, the disappearance of the real separation of two points. As soon as one grasps what is essential and characteristic in discrete space and what differentiates it from continuous space, one must understand why it is necessary for the size of the direct contact of two points to equal one.[35]

Another argument demonstrates directly that the size of the unreal middle point cannot equal zero. It is the argument, cited already by Aristotle, against space being composed of points. That argument says: if simple points which have no parts are in touch with one another, they must touch one another entirely, and in that case they must need coincide, that is to say, they

---

[35]*Über die Grösse,* etc., pp. 242-244.

cannot be distinct spatial points. Petronijevic thoroughly examines the accuracy of that argument applied to real points. Points A and B must coincide, if one supposes their distance equal to zero, because they do not have extremities aimed in different directions. The simple and absolutely indivisible point has no parts at all; in that point, one cannot distinguish different extremities because they would mean just as many different parts of the point. The accuracy of this conclusion can never be verified by the senses, because we cannot perceive a simple and real spatial point, but that accuracy is evident and clear to our reason. When several points are put around another point, it seems at first glance that one can distinguish on that point various sides and various extremities, aimed in the directions of the surrounding points. But that is an illusion: the simple point in itself does not have different sides and different directions; these appear merely in the spatial complex and are nothing other than various relationships existing between simple points. The simple point in itself appears as a whole in any similar relationship, because, being indivisible in itself, it cannot contain such differences. This being established, it is beyond doubt that the size of the unreal middle point between the real central points A and B cannot equal zero, because, in that case, the two points would touch each other entirely, that is to say, they would coincide and no longer be distinct points. The size of the unreal middle point must, therefore, equal one. The real point cannot take the place of the unreal point for the simple reason that the distance of that middle point from each one of two points would then equal zero; the middle point, therefore, would have to coincide with them; these two points, therefore, would also have to coincide.[36]

Bruno conquered the difficulty raised by Aristotle by distinguishing two kinds of points, the minima and the termini. But, by his supposition of the size of the terminus equalling zero, he introduced a contradiction into the notion of discrete space. For this reason, Bruno had to fill the distances between his minima with empty spaces, with ether; in other words, he had to

---

[36]See *Über die Grösse*, etc., pp. 264-266.

identify the termini with the ether. In order to avoid this, one is forced to suppose that the size of the unreal point equals one.

As we know, Bruno also conquered in principle the difficulty of the diagonal of the square: the points of the diagonal of the square are farther from one another than are the points of the sides; for this reason, the diagonal is longer than the side of the square. But he stayed at the half-way point, having been unable to arrive at a clear conception of the existence of *imaginary contact*. Petronijevic demonstrates, on his part, that the existence of the imaginary contact in discrete space can in no way be denied. We are about to cite in their entirety Petronijevic's somewhat too complicated and abstract deductions on the difference between real and imaginary contact in discrete space, because this difference sheds light upon a fact glimpsed and surmised by Bruno. On the figure below, one can see that,

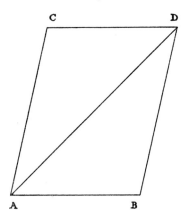

beside the straight lines, the points of which are in direct mutual touch, that is to say, at a distance equalling one, there exists also the straight line at a distance greater than one. The relationship of contact between points A and D is not the same as the relationship of contact between points A and B, A and C, D and C, B and D, C and B. It is incontestable that points A and D are in mutual touch, because a contact relationship must always be supposed where there is no point between two points, and between A and D there is none. Clearly, the *imaginary contact* between A and D would not be possible if the relationship of contact between points A and B, A and C, etc. did not exist. This latter relationship of contact renders possible the givenness of space; that is why Petronijevic calls this relationship *primary contact,* while calling the one between points A and D *secondary contact.* The primary contact he also calls *immediate contact* and the *secondary, mediate contact. Immediate contact is contact unconditioned by surrounding points, and mediate contact is one conditioned by surrounding points.* Consequently, the difference between immediate contact and mediate contact can be reduced to the question of knowing whether or not they are conditioned by points situated around them. The direct relationship of distance between points A and B is absolutely independent of the existence of points situated around them. We can imagine points A and B even without surrounding points, because in that case their relationship of distance would not change at all (see the figure). The mediate relationship of points A and D, by contrast, depends absolutely upon the existence of surrounding points C and B, because points A and D, alone, as numbers of one-dimensional space, could not have this specific relationship of distance; in themselves, they would have, in accordance with their size, the same immediate relationship of distance as the one between points A and B.

The difference between primary contact and secondary contact consists in that the former represents the void while the latter represents pure relationship. If one accepts that the size of the immediate contact equals one, it is clear that this represents the void, and we must suppose that there really is something capable of filling those simple voids in discrete space. As we saw, Petronijevic fills the void between two real points, in mutual touch, with the act of negation outside space.[37] As a metaphysician who takes into consideration the real side of the constitution of space, Petronijevic calls the primary contact *real contact,* because in the purely spatial sense that contact represents negative reality, to which, metaphysically, outside space, there corresponds positive reality, the real act of negation. In-

---

[37]If the act of negation could, in the spatial sense, fill the void between two spatial points, one would obtain a *progressus in infinitum.*

versely, he calls the secondary contact *imaginary contact,* because it does not represent the void; hence, no reality corresponds metaphysically to this contact. "In pure geometry, I use the expressions 'real contact' and 'imaginary contact' above all because, in my capacity as metaphysician, I do not want to forget the relationship between discrete geometry and meta-physics, and these expressions are very convenient for constantly recalling the close relationship between these two disciplines," says Petronijevic.[38]

By establishing a distinction between real and imaginary contact in discrete space, Petronijevic completely eliminates the difficulty of the diagonal of the square; the contact of points in the diagonal is imaginary; hence, greater than one, and for that reason the diagonal of the square is longer than the side of the square. Briefly, by filling the void between two real points in mutual touch by the extra-spatial act of negation, Petronijevic constructed discrete space without resorting to the supposition of empty space between two points in touch, as Bruno did between his minima.

Having taken the size of the minimum to equal one, and the size of the terminus zero, Bruno, in determining the size of a figure, includes in the sum only the minima. *According to Bruno, the size of a figure is equal to the number of its constitutive minima.* Petronijevic, however, establishes with mathematical precision, on the basis of the notion of imaginary contact and by means of Pythagoras' theorem, that *only the unreal points constitute the extension of space.* Consequently, in determining the size of a line or figure in discrete space, it is necessary to take into consideration only the unreal points; the real points should by no means be taken into account; they should be regarded as if they were zeros. Only if the size of the unreal middle point is taken to equal one, and if, in calculating the size of the line, real points are not added together with unreal points, can the contradictions in discrete space disappear.[39]

One must not believe that, with this postulate, discrete

---

[38]*Über die Grösse,* etc., pp. 256-262. See also *Principien der Metaphysik,* pp. 266-269.

[39]See *Über die Grösse,* etc., pp. 246-253.

geometry negates its point of departure. Petronijevic already established that there is no difficulty in the conception of space being composed of points, if only one supposes these points real and their size equal to one. By contrast, he affirms now that the true extension of space does not consist of real points, but only of unreal ones. After all, this last affirmation is not in contradiction with the preceding one; that contradiction could occur only if the size of the real point equalled zero. In view of its being established that the size of the real point must equal one, it immediately becomes clear that the unreal points also must play a role in the extension of space. Moreover, they, *by themselves,* compose the extension of space. At the beginning it seemed that real points, for the very reason that their size equals one, could alone constitute the *expanse* of space, but since it became established that the size of the unreal points equals one, it can be deduced therefrom that only the unreal points constitute that expanse. Petronijevic gives the explanation of this paradoxical fact: the innermost geometrical structure of discrete space is much more complex than it appears at first glance.

In discrete space there are two different constitutive factors: *that which establishes space and that which constitutes it.* Real points are undoubtedly that which establishes space; without them, space could not exist, because unreal points are possible only between real points. Nevertheless, real points are not that which constitutes space itself, the expanse, the very extension of space. For the very reason that they separate the real points, that they represent the closest *distance* between them, the unreal points constitute the extension of discrete space. A single real point does not constitute space at all; it takes two real points to constitute the most elementary space. Two real points being *two* by virtue of the unreal point which separates them, it is, clearly, the unreal point that constitutes the extension of space, that constitutes space.

Having terminated the presentation of Petronijevic's efforts against the fundamental difficulties of discrete geometry, we shall cite all the important passages of his construction of discrete space in general, and of his discrete geometry in particular.

Petronijevic deals with the question of the structure of the discretum without voids, and lays down the following criterion, directly related to all his preceding deductions: kinds of dispositions of points in which the voids separating the points are *greater* than one are impossible, but, kinds of dispositions of points in which these voids are *smaller* than one are also equally impossible. He classifies separately the kinds that fill the discretum without voids. The elementary discrete figure in one-dimensional space is a simple figure with two angles representing the shortest straight line; in two-dimensional space this is the triangle, the quadrangle, the pentagon, and the hexagon; in three-dimensional space, the tetrahedron, the hexahedron, the octahedron and the icosahedron; finally, in four-dimensional space, the pentahedron, the octahedroid, the hexadecahedroid and the icosatetrahedroid. Among these elementary figures the figure with two angles fills the one-dimensional space without voids, the triangle and the square (by reducing the hexagon to triangles) fill, without voids, the two-dimensional space; the three-dimensional space is filled only with the hexahedron (the cube), and the four-dimensional space with the octahedroid and the hexadecahedroid (the icosatetrahedroid can be reduced to the octahedroid). Space with more than four dimensions cannot be filled with any regular figure. In connection with this question Petronijevic establishes the difference, existent only in discrete geometry, between *inextensive space* and *extensive space*. All the points of inextensive space are in direct mutual touch. That space can have an indefinite number of dimensions, while extensive space, identical with simple space, can have no more than four dimensions.

One should recall the existence of rational and of irrational straight lines in discrete space. Although the antagonism between the imaginary and the real does not coincide with the antagonism between the irrational and the rational, only imaginary straight lines can be irrational straight lines, while real straight lines can be taken only for rational straight lines. There are two principal kinds of imaginary straight lines in discrete space. The first kind comprises the straight lines commensurable with one another and with real lines; in the second are imaginary straight lines not commensurable with one another, or with real straight lines: these are the imaginary irrational straight lines. In the absolute continuum, rational and irrational lines coincide, just as, in this continuum, a straight line becomes a circle. Discrete geometry alone can explain irrational lines. About curves, by contrast, discrete geometry cannot teach us, because they are not geometrical factors independent of the constitution of space. Curves can be conceived only in continuous space. In the strict sense, geometrical figures are not possible in the *absolutely* continuous space. One speaks of figures in continuous space because one confuses the notion of the continuum with the notion of the discretum with voids. Geometrical figures in themselves belong to the discretum with voids. Continuous geometry is actually based on the metaphysical hypothesis of the duality of empty space and discrete matter. Petronijevic's previously cited investigations have destroyed this hypothesis, by demonstrating the impossibility of empty space, spatial continuum and infinite discretum. Consequently, continuous geometry loses its importance, and discrete geometry becomes the only geometry logically possible.

We shall likewise present the solution Petronijevic gives to problems of non-Euclidean geometry. By non-Euclidean geometries should be understood, on the one hand, the enlargement of plane space in relation to the number of dimensions (the hypothesis of space with *n* dimensions) and, on the other, the hypothesis of curved spatial forms, which is more important. The enlargement of Euclidean geometry in this second sense refers to the fifth postulate or eleventh axiom of Euclid's *Elements*, the axiom of parallels. It has been shown that there are spaces to which this axiom does not apply, that is to say, spaces in which from a point outside a given straight line one can draw several parallels, or cannot draw any (spaces in which the sum of the angles of a triangle is greater or smaller than 180°). These are, first of all, surfaces with positive and negative curvature, the surfaces of the sphere (Riemann), and of the pseudosphere (Lobachevski). The space of Riemann, as well as the one of Lobachevski, is as indeterminate in relation to the number of dimensions as the space of Euclid. Among mathematicians there is controversy as to the value of non-Euclidean geometry in the realm of the real. The adversaries of this geometry affirm that the space of our experience has no curvatures and that the non-Euclidean spaces are special constructions of Euclid's general space (the interior of the sphere, as well as that of the pseudosphere, is filled with empty space which is Euclidean). According to Petronijevic, empty space requires the existence of real matter scattered in it; for this reason the pretensions of non-Euclidean geometry become more serious. One might suppose with Mill that in various regions of the universe different laws prevail, determining the order of the particles of matter; in that case, one could imagine various spatial forms of that order. Really, the new geometry is a logical consequence of the ancient geometry of Euclid, because curved geometrical forms can be deduced directly from the most important principle of ancient geometry, the principle of infinity. Discrete geometry alone, which broke with the notion of infinity, rejects, by this very rupture, the non-Euclidean spatial figures, and establishes the possibility of a single geometry, the Euclidean geometry.

In his work *De Triplici Minimo*, Bruno, who did not know the non-Euclidean geometries, underscores in a very persuasive manner the uselessness of enlarging the propositions of Euclid by the rules of spherical triangles. According to Bruno, geometry will not become more fertile by a multiplication of propositions. The point of contact in this question between Bruno and Petronijevic consists in their aspiration toward a simplification of geometry, an aspiration motivated in Bruno by an instinctive belief, by a sort of intuition, and based in Petronijevic on conscious knowledge powerfully illuminated by the progress of mathematical sciences since realized. Both firmly believe that only in this manner can one establish the relationship between geometry and metaphysics.

Petronijevic also removes a difficulty of a purely psychological and empirical nature that can be raised against discrete geometry. According to the new geometry, all curvilinear forms and a number of rectilinear geometrical figures are impossible, but they are perceived just as well as the forms which, according to this geometry, are possible. The reason for this is to be found in the fact that a real spatial point in itself cannot be perceived. Only complexities of real points, which points are equal among themselves and qualitatively different from other surrounding points, can be perceived. This explains also the fact of a distinct perception of a circular line.

The last elements of space being imperceptible, the knowledge of whether space is to be conceived as discrete or as continuous depends on purely logical reasons. The logical reasons speak for discrete space. Moreover, if space is discrete, it can very easily be understood why it is not perceived as discrete, and why it is perceived as discrete only in *some* of its parts; while in the case of continuous space, the very impossibility of perceiving its infinitely small parts remains inexplicable, together with the fact of a discrete perception of some of its parts.[40]

We are proceeding to the exposition of Petronijevic's discrete geometry. This geometry is composed of three parts. The first sets forth the geometry of one-dimensional space and of two-dimensional space; the second presents the geometry of three-dimensional space; and, finally, the third part deals with the geometry of four dimensions. Petronijevic explains the essence and the relationships of the simplest geometrical figures in the form of definitions, axioms, and theorems.

Among the definitions we shall cite those that are of special importance from the point of view of discrete geometry:

1. A *point* is the last part of space, a part simple and indivisible.

2. A *central point* is a real point filled with matter.

3. A *middle point* is an unreal, empty point.

4. Two central points are in *mutual touch* when they are not separated by a third central point.

5. Two central points are in *immediate or real mutual* touch, when they are separated by a middle point.

6. Two central points are in *mediate or imaginary mutual touch,* when the distance of their contact does not coincide with the middle point.

---

[40]*Principien der Metaphysik*, S 256-307.

7. *Inextensive* space is the one all the points of which are in direct mutual touch.

8. *Extensive* space is the one all the points of which are not in direct mutual touch.

9. *Direction* is the relationship of succession of two points one of which *precedes* and the other *follows*.

10. *Dimension* is the primary direction of extension of spatial points, that is to say, the direction which determines space.

11. A *dimension* of *inextensive* space is every direction of the extension of its points, starting from one of these points.

12. The *dimension* of *extensive* space is that of its extension, which derives its origin from the dimensional direction of extension of inextensive space; this direction being the origin of extensive space.

13. A *line* is a system or sequence of points in which the points are in mutual touch, two by two.

14. The *straight line* or space with one dimension is a line in which every point is in touch only with a preceding point.

15. A *broken line* is a line in which every point is in touch with two or more preceding points.

16. The contact distance of two points in mutual touch is the simplest line or an *elementary straight line*.

17. The *elementary straight line* is *real* when the distance of its contact is real.

18. The *elementary straight line* is *imaginary* when the distance of its contact is imaginary.

19. A *line* is *real* when it is composed of real elementary straight lines.

20. A *line* is *imaginary* when it is composed of imaginary contact distances or of imaginary and real contact distances.

21. Two *straight lines* are of *the same kind* when they are composed of homogeneous elementary straight lines.

22. Two *straight lines* are of *different kinds* when they are composed of heterogeneous elementary straight lines.

23. An imaginary empty interstice, enclosed either by *three* points in direct mutual touch, or by *four* points, two of which are in real mutual touch, and two in the imaginary, is the simplest

surface or *elementary plane*. In the first case, the elementary plane is a *simple triangle*, in the second, a *simple square*.

24. An *extended plane* is a system of straight lines in which every straight line is in touch with a single preceding straight line.

25. A *triangular plane* is a plane composed of triangles, that is to say, one which represents a system of points in which the points are in direct mutual touch, three by three, or in which every point is surrounded by six points. The *surrounding points* are those closest to a point.

26. A *square plane* is a plane composed of simple squares, or one which represents a system of points in which every point is surrounded by eight points.

27. Two *straight lines meet* either when they intersect at a point, or when they closely cross over one another without intersecting.

28. An *angle* is the difference between the directions of two straight lines that meet. When the straight lines intersect at a point, that point of intersection is called the *apex of the angle;* the straight lines of the angle are called, in all cases, its *sides.*

29. An *angle* is *real* when it is composed of real straight lines.

30. An *angle* is *imaginary* when one or both sides are imaginary straight lines.

31. An *elementary angle* is the first real angle, constructed by two real straight lines in a plane.

35. Two *angles* are *qualitatively equal* when they are composed of homogeneous straight lines.

36. Two *angles* are *qualitatively unequal* when they are composed of heterogeneous straight lines.

37. A *simple angle*, from the qualitative point of view, is one which cannot be decomposed into simpler angles of the same kind, or one between the sides of which no straight line can be drawn, that would be qualitatively equal to one of the sides or to both sides.

38. A *composite angle*, from the qualitative point of view, is one that can be decomposed into several simpler angles,

between which there are angles of the same kind as the given angle, or in which all the angles obtained are of that same kind.

41. A *figure* is *real* when its sides are real.

42. A *figure* is *imaginary* when all its sides are imaginary straight lines, or when amid its sides there are also imaginary straight lines.

43. A *figure perceived by the senses*, which cannot be geometrically justified, more precisely, which cannot be constructed, is *impossible*.

In Petronijevic's discrete geometry there are nine axioms:

1. Space is composed of points.

2. The number of spatial points is finite.

3. The point is a simple and quantitatively indivisible unit.

4. There are two kinds of points: real, central points and unreal, middle points.

5. The unreal, middle points represent the extension of space, and the real, central points, that which is given in space.

6. Two points in mutual touch are in opposite directions in relation to each other.

7. $N + 1$ points in direct mutual touch represent inextensive space with n dimensions.

8. Extensive space derives its origin from inextensive space.

9. That which is placed in qualitatively the same manner is also quantitatively equal.

In his hypermetaphysics Petronijevic gives a definitive solution to the problem of the discrete nature of space, that is to say, of its being composed of simple points. There he deduces directly from the notion of the simple real point that two points touching each other in an absolutely immediate fashion cannot constitute a simple spatial line, it being necessary to conceive their relationship in this case as non-spatial. Only if three points are placed in such a fashion that one point touches the other two in an absolutely immediate manner, while the latter two points are not in such a contact relationship, in other words, only if two points are not in mutual touch in an absolutely immediate manner, can these points constitute a spatial line. This deduction removes all the difficulties encountered by the fundamental hypotheses of discrete space in the domain of metaphysics.

We have seen that in his metaphysical construction of discrete space Petronijevic filled the simple void that separates two real points, in direct mutual touch in the spatial sense, with an extra-spatial act of negation. In his hypermetaphysics, he determines the relationship of the point of negation to the two points it separates. The relationship of the point of negation to each of the two real points of space is imagined by Petronijevic as an empty extra-spatial point. The simple point, situated between two real points in direct mutual touch (that is to say, between the real act of negation, on the one hand, and each of the real points separated by it, on the other), differs essentially from the unreal empty point, situated between two points in direct mutual touch in space, in that the latter represents the void in space while the former does not. From that, one can conclude at once that the absolute size of the two points cannot be the same. If the size of the unreal spatial point equals *one* in the absolute sense, then the size of the unreal extra-spatial point must be supposed to equal zero. By contrast, if the size of the unreal extra-spatial point is equal to the absolutely simple unit (one), then the size of the unreal spatial point equals *a multiplicity of units*. From the hypermetaphysical point of view, only the second part of the alternative can be accepted as true; the unreal point outside space is a *point*, and, as such, it unquestionably has a size (its size equals one). It should be stressed that, for Petronijevic, the unreal extra-spatial point represents the *absolutely* simple point; this point is a pure relationship, absolutely without matter, whereas the real point is simple only in the extensive sense, and infinitely divisible only in the intensive sense.[41] Petronijevic supposes the existence of a relationship of distance without direction between the extra-spatial point of negation and the two spatial points separated by it, having already demonstrated the logical possibility of that relationship. When, however, the two spatial points occur in a certain direction in relation to each other, their simultaneity must be a simple spatial relationship of distance. By its function of separation, the extra-spatial

---

[41]Petronijevic takes the point to be an intensive continuum, potentially divisible to infinity. Likewise, he conceives of a real point of world substance as such a continuum.

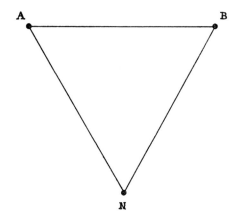

point of negation makes the two points occur not only *outside each other*, but also in a *determinate direction* in relation to each other. Point N represents the extra-spatial point of negation, points A and B represent real spatial points, separated by it. While lines NA and NB represent the relationship of distance without direction, line AB represents the simple relationship of direction; as such, it must be treated as a simple geometrical unit. There is, then, a difference between this geometrical unit and the relationship of distance without direction which is a pure arithmetical unit. The difference consists in that the size of the unreal spatial middle point equals two absolute units, in other words, in that two spatial points situated close to each other are in a relationship of distance equalling two absolute units. Thus, by interposing two relationships of contact without direction between three real points, Petronijevic achieves his hypermetaphysical deduction of the simple spatial line. As a result, it becomes clear that the shortest spatial distance in discrete space must of necessity equal two absolute units; putting it differently, in the entire network of real points, by which discrete space is ontologically conditioned, no distance without direction can be greater than the absolute unit.

Perhaps this deduction of so rigorous a dialectic was present as an intuitive hunch in Bruno's consciousness when he asserted that the minima do not touch each other through one common terminus, but through two termini.

By means of this deduction, Petronijevic removes the two

principal difficulties encountered by discrete geometry in the domain of metaphysics, namely, the difficulty of the void that represents the unreal point in discrete space, and the difficulty presented by the impossibility of adding together empty spatial points with real points.

Here, the unreal spatial point no longer represents the void in the sense in which it was understood in the preceding arguments. If its size were identical with the size of the real point, if that size equalled an absolute unit, we could, then, affirm, if we wanted to keep the real act of negation, that the distance between the unreal spatial point and each of the two real points equals zero. In that case, this point would have to be situated in space itself, and discrete space would thus be abolished. If, on the other hand, we wanted to negate the act of negation, then the unreal spatial point would represent a void within being itself, which is impossible. The difficulty disappears in the twinkling of an eye, if we suppose that the empty spatial point equals two absolute units. In that case, it no longer represents the void in the sense that a real point can fill it, but only in the sense that real points could be shifted and pulled even closer to each other: down to the absolutely simple and nonspatial distance, equal to one, if the real act of negation did not exist.

The second difficulty in the realm of metaphysics Petronijevic resolves by showing the qualitative difference between two kinds of points in space. For the metaphysician as well as for the mathematician, it is enough to imagine this qualitative difference in an act of self-transport; for the hypermetaphysician, seeking the ultimate logical reasons, this is not enough. Because the hypermetaphysician asks himself why it is impossible to disregard this qualitative difference between points, seeing that, in the process of addition, only their qualitative structure is taken into consideration. The difficulty is removed as soon as one supposes the size of the unreal spatial point equal to two units. The spatial distance of the unit, represented by the unreal spatial point, on the one hand, and the real spatial point, on the other, cannot be compared with one another in relation to their concrete size, because the former is worth two absolute units and the latter only one; in other words, because the size of the latter, compared to that of the former, represents zero, which is to say, that it is without size.[42]

Thus, we have given in its entirety Petronijevic's construction of discrete space.

In closing, it remains for us to mention that Petronijevic, starting from his arguments against the infinity of space and from the elementary propositions of his doctrine of space, carries to its ultimate logical implications the theory of the finiteness of the universe in contrast with Bruno who, despite his doctrine of the minimum, proclaimed the infinity of the universe.

Our exposition of the metaphysical and geometrical doctrine of Petronijevic seems to us to have shown sufficiently that only four centuries after the death of Bruno, his fertile ideas, now and again of genius, but confused and chaotic, have at last been corrected and developed to their ultimate implications within a logical system. Bruno's doctrine of the minimum, forgotten and neglected, partly because it took a direction different from that of the development of most conceptions of space, partly because of its extremely confused composition, has had two remarkable adherents: first Leibniz, then Petronijevic. Between Bruno's attempt to construct discrete geometry and Petronijevic's construction of the same geometry, the difference is as great as between Bruno's doctrine of the monad and Leibniz's Monadology. This is why, in discrete geometry, the Philosopher from Nola is of importance mainly as a precursor of Petronijevic.

But since the value of later doctrines is the best argument in favor of the one which was the first to appear, it was obviously worthwhile to decipher the laborious hieroglyphs of Bruno's style and ideas, as much because Bruno's doctrine has thereby been historically connected with a more perfect system, similar in its fundamental idea, as for the very lesson that can be drawn from that doctrine.

---

[42]See B. Petronievics, *Principien der Metaphysik*, Erster Band, Zweite Abtheilung, Die realen Kategorien und die letzten Principien, Heidelberg, 1912, pp. 432-447.

INDEX*

A

Absolute minimum, 46, *see also*
   Minimum in genus
Abstract concepts, faculty of, 23
Accent, minimum of, 47
Achilles' movement, Zeno's argument
   against, 44
Activity, source of, 26
Act of negation, 115, 131
Addition, xvii, xxiii, 34 and *passim*
Adler, xii
Affection, minimum of, 47
Allegorical interpretations, 88 and
   passim
Anatomist, 46
Anaxagoras, 12, 13, 43
Anaximenes, 91
Angle, arc, chord, center, circle,
   circumference, diameter, radius
   and straight line, 29-34 and *passim*
Angles, 29-34, 49, 65, 71, 72, 78, 92,
   93 and *passim*
Animals, 45, 56, 62 and *passim*
Anthropological implications, 22, 23,
   46, 47, 54-57, 62-64
Anti-Semitism, xi
Antiphon, 65, 66
apeiron, 5, 6
aporias, Zeno's, 10
Appollonius of Tyana, xiii
Approximation in practice, Bruno's
   views of, 66, 68
Arab scholastics (the Mutakallimun),
   xxvi, 17-19
Arc, 29-34, 66, 82-84 and *passim*
   and chord, 31, 32
   division of, 82
   largest and smallest, 32
Archaeopteryx, *see* Petronijevic, vi
Aristophanes, xix
Aristotle, xii, xvi, xviii, xix, xxiii, 3-8,
11, 14-17, 19, 36, 38-40, 42-44, 51,
95, 98, 102, 107, 116, 117
Arithmetic, Pythagorean, 9
Arnim, 15, 17
Art (skill), 45 and *passim*
artioperitton, 5
Astronauts, xv
Astonomy, xv-xvii, xx, xxiii, xxiv and
   passim
   ancient, xx
   cosmocentric, xx
   modern, xvii
Atanasijevic, Ksenija (Atanassievitch,
   Xénia), v-xii, xxii
   bibliography of, xii, xiii
Athens, xi
Atomic theory, contemporary, xviii
Atomism and atomists, xvi, xvii, xix,
   13-17, 19
   materialist, 48
   mathematical, 17, 100
   mathematico-physical, 100
   physical, 100
   purely metaphysical, 18
Atoms, xvii, xviii, xxii, 14, 26, 33, 34,
   36, 45, 59, 69, 70, 88, 101, 105,
   and *passim*
Augustinus, Aurelius, xiii
Authority, 23 and *passim*
Axis powers, Yugoslavia's occupation
   by, xi

B

Bartholmess, 22
Becquerel, Henri, xviii
Being, 9, 10, 12, 30, 131, and *passim*
Belgrade (Beograd), v, vi, xi, xii
   Académie Royale Serbe, vi
   National Library, xii
   Serbian Academy, xi
   University of, vi, xi

133

---

* For technical reasons beyond the translator's control, the diacritical signs
at the end of Slavic proper names could not be shown. Readers familiar with
Serbo-Croatian will know where these signs belong, and those unfamiliar will
not miss them.

C

D

E

H

J

K

L

N

O

P

Q

R

minimum of, 47
perception by, 83
See also Intellect, Intelligence,
    Perception
Reasoning, philosophical, 23
Reasons, "bread of better and stronger,"
    58-59
Reasons, logical, ultimate, 131
Rectangular triangle, *see* Triangle,
    rectangular
Rectilinear and curvilinear forms, 124-
    125 and *passim; see also* Geometry,
    discrete
Rectilinear triangle, *see* Triangle,
    rectilinear
Reflections on man, *see* Anthropological
    implications
Relative vs. absolute, 55
Relativism, cultural and individual,
    54-56
Relativity of:
    esthetic, ethical and gustatory—
        olfactory reactions, 54-56, 87
    sensory perception, 54-56
Renaissance, greatest thinker of, v, xv
Riemann, *see* Non-Euclidean Geometry,
    123
Right angle, constancy of, 86
Robin, xi
Rome, xxi
Rose, Lynn, ix
Rules, proliferation of, 83; *see also*
    Propositions, multiplication of
Rutherford, xviii

S

Salvestrini, Virgilio, vii
Sayings and words, 23, 24, 26, 55 and
    passim
Schelling, xx, xxiv
Schmidt, Sandee, x
Scholasticism, dogmas of, xx
Scholastics, Arab, *see* Arab scholastics
Schopenhauer, xiii
Sciences, classification of, 65
Scientific method, *see* Method
Scolia, 20, 21, 69, 82 and *passim*

Seasons, four, recurrence of in infinity,
    42
Secondary contact (mediate), 118-120
Self-preservation, desire for, 87
Sensations, 64
Senses (faculties) external, 51, 53-56
Sense (faculty), internal, 54-56
Senses, seeking beyond, 56-59 and
    passim
Sensible form, minimum of, 47
Sensory perception, relativity of, 54-57
    see also Perception
Sensory structures and functions, 23,
    54-57 and *passim*
Sensory verification, 117
Serbo-Croatian (Croato-Serbian),
    translations into, xii
Shock and movement, minimum of, 44
Sight and hearing, sensations of, 64
Similarities, endurance of, 86-87
Simple/composite *see* Substance and
    accident
Skinner, Margo, x
Smallest, *see* Minimum
Smallest line, defined, 89
Smallest/largest, 25, 30, 31, 34 and
    passim;
    identical, 25, 30
    interconditional, 34
    see also Minimum/maximum
Smallest terminus, 47
Socrates, xii, xxiv, 65
Solids, 4-7, and *passim;*
    see also Mathematical and physical
        atomism
Sophists, xii, 21, 75 and *passim*
Soul, 27-29, 56, 58, 59, 63, 64 and
    passim;
    as circle, 29
    as indivisible spiritual substance, 28
    hunger of, 56, 58-59
    immortality of, 27, 28
    nature of, 63
    of souls, 64
Space and time, continuous/
    discontinuous, 12 and *passim*
Space, conceptions and theories of,
    106-107
Space, continuous, xviii, xxvi, 9-13, 16,

X

Y

Z